C000172167

The Gh.

The Cuban Queen

Bordello

A story of a 1920s

Jerome, Arizona Madam

By Peggy Hicks

Editing and cover design by

Dennis Andrews

Published By: Peggy Hicks
Distributed by: Arizona Discoveries
Jerome, Arizona, 86331

ISBN 978-0-578-07343-9

First Printing 2011
Printed in the United States of America

To obtain a copy of this paperback contact
Arizona Discoveries
317 Main St.
Jerome, Arizona 86331
928-634-5716
azdiscoveries@swiftaz.net

Resources, References, Acknowledgments and Illustrations

The Jerome Historical Society Archives
Jerome, Arizona

Nancy Smith- Collection
Jerome, Arizona Historian

Professor George Hall Collection
Jerome, Arizona

Louise Giusto
Consultant, Jerome, Arizona

Mike Ford- Collection
The Cuban Queen's grandson

Helen J. Stewart- Collection
University of Nevada, Las Vegas

William Russell
Historic New Orleans- Collection

Dead Man Blues: Jelly Roll Morton Way Out West
Phil Pastras

Station KHMU-Fm 94.7 Radio Broadcast (1950s)
Bob Kirstein

Jelly Blues, Life, Music, & Redemption
Howard Reich and Williams Gaines

Untold Story of Jelly Roll Morton Last Years
Floyd Levin

Ghost of Cleopatra Hill (1994)
They Came to Jerome (1972)
Herbert V. Young

Doctor Jazz
International Researchers

Peggy Hicks Collection
Author's personal photos and illustrations

JEROME. ARIZ.

Jerome Arizona

Jerome, Arizona, once known as *The Wickedest Town in the West*, was named after a New York City banker and philanthropist named *Eugene Murray Jerome*. His cousin was, *Jenny Jerome*, the mother of the former Prime Minister of the United Kingdom, *Winston Churchill*. Although Eugene Jerome was a major investor in the town's copper mining operation, he never made a single visit to his namesake town.

Jerome was founded in 1876, and established a post office in 1883. In 1899, shortly after four devastating fires destroyed large portions of the town, Jerome was incorporated.

Jerome began as a small copper mining camp consisting of nothing more than a few tents and some crudely built shacks. Successful mining caused the camp to grow and soon, Jerome became well known not only for its mining, but also for its gambling, brothels, and saloons. Inside these establishments, one could find many different types of men, but only one kind of woman.

During the town's glory days, the miner's shifts ran around the clock. When they were not working the miles of underground tunnels that honeycombed the earth beneath the town, they were raising hell in the many bars and bordellos. The town boasted of 13 hotels, 21 bars, and 8 houses of prostitution with names like *The Cuban Queen, Belgian Jenny's,* and the less elegant *Cribs*.

With the population consisting of over 90% men, Jerome sometimes became a violent place. Gambling became epidemic and it was said that most men carried a deck of cards in their pocket and a revolver in their boot. By the 1920's the town's population had grown to over fifteen thousand. When the Great Depression hit Jerome, copper prices plummeted and production slowed to a crawl. The once precious metal became too expensive to mine and too cheap to sell. As a result, hundreds of men found themselves jobless.

It was during the '30's that a dynamite blasts combined with general shifting caused parts of the town to crack and slide. One afternoon a particularly powerful blast caused the unstable town to tremble and portions of the town's buildings were lost in a massive landslide. In an instant, a whole block slid down to the next level of town. Most of the buildings in the red-light section were completely demolished and then buried under fifty feet of earth and debris. The town's jailhouse was a well-constructed building of heavy concrete and steel, and somehow held together as it slid two hundred twenty-five feet downhill, and came to rest on the street below. Ironically, the *Sliding Jail* ended up in the red-light district. Some townspeople thought this was quite fitting since most of the crimes were committed in that area of town anyway. *The Cuban Queen Bordello* received only slight damage, however, two wooden structures that were attached to the building gave way and came crashing to the ground in a heap of rubble.

In 1935, Phelps Dodge Mining Corp. purchased the United Verde Copper Company for $22,800,000.00, but the mine was forced to close in 1938. World War II brought prosperity back for a while, but the inevitable end of mining in Jerome was near.

In 1953, Phelps Dodge ceased all operations permanently. The Jerome population quickly dwindled as miners went looking for work in other mines around the state and beyond. Jerome soon became nothing more than just another ghost town. Shutters banged against buildings, doors creaked with the wind and what wasn't nailed down was stripped away by looters and vandals. Doors, windows, bathtubs, furniture and in some cases entire houses were hauled away. Then, some concerned citizens formed the Jerome Historical Society. Their main purpose was to preserve Jerome's downtown section.

By the early 1960s, fewer than fifty souls remained in the town. One of the few businesses to remain open was *Paul and Jerry's Saloon.* Paul and Jerry's is still open today and boasts of being the oldest family owned and operated saloon in Arizona.

In 1967, Jerome was designated a historic district and in 1976, it became a national historic landmark.

Jerome had begun its leisurely journey back to life. Slowly, new entrepreneurs rediscovered Jerome and by the early 1970's, merchants sent spooks scurrying as they took over a few of the old abandoned buildings. Main Street was soon lined with cute little gift shops where visitors could shop for trinkets, rock samples and souvenirs. Travelers could grab a bite to eat at the *English Kitchen*, load up with Indian jewelry at the *Turquoise Spider* jewelry store and get their sugar fixes on some rich chocolate fudge from the *Copper Country Fudge Shop*.

When darkness fell, the streets were again vacant, making way for the shy spirits to step out from the shadows to play. By the mid 1990s, Jerome was a full-fledged travel destination for tourists, bikers, and rock hounds alike.

Today, Jerome has a wide range of unique gift shops, art galleries restaurants, wine tasting rooms and watering holes that some claim are still inhabited by ghosts from the past. Jerome also has a bustling nightlife with live music, restaurants open for dinner, art walks and ghost hunting tours armed with *EMF* detectors and digital cameras searching for any strange paranormal activity.

Las Vegas

Lake Powell

Grand Canyon

Williams Flagstaff

Sedona Winslow

Jerome
Prescott MOGOLLON RIM

Lake Havasu Payson

Glendale Scottsdale

Phoenix

San Diego

Yuma

Tucson

Rocky Point

Bisbee

The *Ghost* of the Cuban Queen Bordello

A story of a 1920s
Jerome, Arizona Madam

By Peggy Hicks

To My Children and Grandchildren,

Have a clear vision of what you want in life and keep your desires and actions on the same page.

Contents

Preface

After an unsettling, modern-day ghostly encounter, the author, through years of research, uncovers the secret life and deplorable deeds of an attractive, but devious Madam once known as The Cuban Queen.

This Madam began her trade in the early 1900s in the red-light district of Storyville, New Orleans. While married in the early 1920s to the famous Jelly Roll Morton, (*the self-proclaimed inventor of jazz*), they traveled the country helping to set trends in both fashion and music during the infancy of the jazz age.

With their somewhat toxic relationship in tow, these cunning lovers and business partners owned and operated a hotel and nightclub in Los Angeles, California, and then a jazz club in San Francisco. After a few years of marriage and several vicious breakups, they finally parted ways permanently. Jelly Roll Morton went east in search of fame and The Queen went west in search of wealth.

One of her stops was Jerome, Arizona, one of the world's richest copper mining towns. During the celebrated Roaring Twenties, this buxom harlot, known to the locals only as The Cuban Queen, ruled for a decade in this rough and tumble Arizona mining town.

Old timers of Jerome, remembered her as a dark skinned, curvaceous, well-dressed madam, possibly *mulatto*, who spoke with a pronounced southern accent. Some said she was a little mysterious and rumor had it that she was deeply rooted in the practice of the *voodoo* traditions.

An anonymous source said, *"Her place was known as The Cuban Queen Boarding House, but most everyone knew what it really was. One thing was for sure. If the pretty girls didn't keep you coming back, her fine southern cooking would. A lot went on behind the closed doors of The Cuban Queen's place. Prostitution, gambling, bootlegged whiskey and God knows what else went on in there. It was a rather popular place, but, very high-priced."*

Late one night in 1927, one of The Cuban Queen's working girls, *Guadalupe Villalpando,* was found murdered in her own bed just feet from witnesses, yet no one dared to step forward. This cunning madam and her handsome accomplice, *John Ford,* kidnapped the dead girl's baby boy, and by the light of a full August moon, slipped out of town, never to be heard from again. For years, the family of the missing boy searched for their lost baby brother, to no avail. Now, almost 80 years later, the jury is in.

Follow the twists and turns as the writer tells the rest of the story, revealing what became of the kidnapped boy, Jelly Roll Morton, and the mysterious madam once known as "The Cuban Queen".

Chapter 1

The Haunted Bordello

The Cuban Queen Bordello at 324 Queen Street, Jerome, Az

Did I really see a ghost? What else could it have been? I'll surely never forget that crisp November morning at the old Cuban Queen Bordello.

My day started as a typical Monday morning and for about the past hour, I had been drinking coffee and listening to a guest speaker at our weekly real estate office meeting. I had been a real estate agent in the area for many years and the list of things that I needed to accomplish that day, seemed a mile long. My first priority that brisk November morning was to preview several properties for an out-of town client. The potential buyer was interested in a property in the small nearby historic town of Jerome. I made a quick call to the listing office to get permission to show the property. They told me that the owner was selling the lots only and would not guarantee the existing structure. They said the old building was in such disrepair, that more than likely it would eventually have to be demolished. I had previously sold property in Jerome and was aware of the steep hillsides and rocky terrain. I stopped by my house and traded in my slacks and heels for a pair of blue jeans and tennis shoes. I made sure to grab my camera and then began the drive up the steep vertical winding road to Jerome. As I pulled up to the address, 324 Queen Street, there was a *KEEP OUT* sign  posted on the boarded-up front door and the real estate *FOR SALE* sign had been knocked over. I gave a half-hearted effort to straighten it up, but the metal stake was bent and twisted. This particular property had been on and off the market several times over the years. It had been terribly neglected but somehow, had continued to preserve its somewhat intriguing character.

Known to the locals as *The Cuban Queen Bordello,* it was built in the early 1920s, replacing a flimsy wooden shack destroyed by one of Jerome's many historic fires. Peeking inside through a glassless window frame as my eyes adjusted to the darkness, I could see the interior lay in complete ruins. A few small fragments of red velvet wallpaper were still clinging

defiantly to the interior wall of the parlor. The pine floorboards were rotted, and many had fallen into the lower story. The face of the building was originally painted a rich apricot color, but many decades in the Arizona sun had faded it to almost a chalky white color. The copper trim, once polished to a brilliant shine, was now tarnished to a dull blue-green patina. The sun-bleached building stood alone on the deserted street. This once sturdy structure of brick and stone was now crumbling. Its foundation was failing and large stress cracks were evident. Back in her prime, The Cuban Queen Bordello must have sparkled like a diamond in a royal crown and surely would have seemed out of place among the hastily built wooden shacks that accompanied 'Her Highness' there on Queen Street. Inquisitively, I made my way down through the rubble on the adjacent lot to access the back of the building. All of the windowpanes were broken and shattered glass was everywhere. The ornate balcony, once attached to the upper story had fallen to its demise many years prior, and a number of its decorative spindles were scattered among the debris. Remnants of a wide wooden staircase leading to an upper  story balcony were still standing. At the top of the staircase was a landing that once housed a communal bathroom and an obvious addition to the original building. Crude plumbing was hanging from beneath a cast-iron claw-foot bathtub. A wire-reinforced window stood balanced in a rotted frame. It looked as if the whole contraption could fall through the floor at any moment. The lower half of the building had several small rooms known as *cribs*, each with a door to the outside.

(Cribs were small, narrow rooms rented by prostitutes and arranged for a quick turn over. The women often lived and worked in these tiny rooms. Typically, these rooms, were sparsely furnished, with a single bed, a chair, and a stand with a washbowl.

One of the little rooms had a door that was stuck in the dirt and standing partly open. Peeking through the opening, I could see a rusty bed frame up against the far wall. I foolishly began to squeeze through the doorway to explore further, but quickly changed my mind. There was no telling what type of vermin might take refuge in a place like this. Rats, spiders, scorpions or even worse, a rattlesnake could be lurking about in the shadows just waiting for its next victim. Just getting back there would have been dangerous, taking into account the condition of the crumbling structure.

Discarding the thought of going inside, I walked to the edge of the lot and noticed the newly surveyed corners were clearly marked with fresh wooden stakes and pink plastic florescent ribbons. From this vantage point the view was spectacular. Looking northwest, the San Francisco Peaks were covered in early snow. From there the landscape swept across the warm sculptured red rocks of Sedona.

Suddenly, feeling a little weak in the knees, I sat down on a crumbling rock wall to catch my breath. As I sat there quietly, a rather peaceful feeling washed over me. Then I heard a small child calling in Spanish. The faint cry stopped and then repeated, *"Donde esta mi mama Lupe?"* I could also faintly hear music playing in the background. It sounded like one of those old scratchy phonograph recordings of a piano playing some sort of old jazz tune.

As I looked around for its source, I swore I smelled fried chicken. Both the smell and the music seemed to be coming from the old dilapidated Cuban Queen Bordello. I knew that it was impossible, for someone to be living in there. Then, looking up, I could hardly believe my eyes. I sat frozen as I got a glimpse of a woman seemingly standing in mid-air right where the upper story balcony once stood. Her image wasn't fuzzy or misty like one would imagine a ghost might look, but on the contrary, quite detailed. The woman looked to be in her mid-thirties. Her black hair was cut into a short bob, like a haircut out of the roaring twenties. She wore a cream-colored chiffon flapper dress with a dropped waistline giving her a tall, straight appearance. This was unlike the women in the Victorian era who wore corsets to give them that coveted hourglass figure. She appeared sophisticated, and all decked out in shimmering diamond jewelry. She looked like someone important, maybe royalty or even a queen. I could see she was wearing excessive makeup and dark red lipstick that shaped her full lips. I noticed a slight sparkle as the apparition gave me a somewhat fake, half grin. Oddly, she was holding a wooden spoon and shaking her head no. I wasn't really frightened, but more bewildered than anything. How was it was possible someone could appear in mid-air like that? Then, she turned and seemed to float right through the solid brick wall on the upper story.

With camera in hand, I scrambled and tried to get a look around the corner hoping to snap a picture, but the figure had simply vanished. I noticed then that the music had stopped and I could no longer smell the fried chicken.

The air was now filled with the fragrance of a sweet rose scented perfume. Feeling a little queasy, I thought to myself, *"Wow, had I just seen a ghost?"*

I had never experienced anything like this before and naturally, I was a bit skeptical. Not wanting to damage my credibility as a real estate professional, I thought, perhaps I had better just keep this all to myself.

Unable to get the image out of my mind, I kicked around among the debris for a while, contemplating how, or even if, I was going to tell anyone about my experience. I spotted an old book lying among the rubbish and bent over to pick it up. It was tattered, swelled and barely held together. As I turned the first page, it practically crumbled in my hands. I noticed an old playing card stuck inside the book and pulled it out. As I rubbed the dirt from the moldy card, I noticed it was the Queen of Clubs. The unsettling part was that the woman on the playing card seemed to resemble the apparition I had just seen. The card slipped from my hand.

A sudden gust of wind picked it up and the card fluttered in the air for a moment before falling to the ground right back at my feet.

I looked around as if to say, "Did you see that?" I bent over, picked up the card again and slid it into my back pocket. I knew I shouldn't make-off with anything from someone else's property, but I couldn't resist. What harm could an old card bring anyway?

Out here in the West, rumor has it if you take an old artifact, relic, or anything else from these abandoned places, bad luck will attach itself to you until you return the item. I hoped that wouldn't be the case. Enough strange things had happened to me that day.

I climbed back up to the top of the hill and looked over my shoulder toward the bordello. *'If walls could only talk, I'll bet these would have quite a story to tell.'* I wondered who the ghostly figure might have been. Maybe she was trying to tell me not to sell the bordello. Maybe she feared her house would be demolished and she wouldn't have any place to go. Honestly, I wasn't sure what to think. The experience was however, the beginning of my mission to find out more about the building, its history, and its ghostly inhabitant.

I started my pursuit to find out more about The Cuban Queen and her bordello with a visit to the town of Jerome archives.

I took this photo in the back of the Cuban Queen Bordello.
The apparition was floating midway up the wall, just about
where the upper story balcony was once attached.

Chapter 2

The Ghost City Archives

Main Street Jerome, Arizona c.1920

I was unsure what fueled my burning curiosity about this woman. Maybe it was the lingering spirit of The Cuban Queen herself. Perhaps it was the uneasy spirits of the many men she had entertained here, or maybe it was just the sight of that ghostly figure that drove me.

Modern day Jerome is a quaint little tourist/artist town balanced on the nearly vertical slopes of Cleopatra Hill. State Highway 89A winds its way up the hill in a series of curves and narrow switchbacks. The current population of this once forgotten town is roughly five hundred people. The streets are lined with charming little gift shops, art galleries, eateries, wineries and old-fashioned saloons. Jerome has become a travel destination for tourists, bikers, and even ghost hunters. Looking at the town today makes it difficult to imagine that at one time this now small community boasted a population of fifteen thousand residents.

By the 1920s, Jerome was the fourth largest city in Arizona. The town's well-known red-light district had been a stone's throw from Main Street, and The Cuban Queen Bordello is one of the few buildings remaining in that district. [1]Most of the other buildings were destroyed and are now just memories.

Shortly after the mines closed in the early 1950s, the Phelps Dodge Mining Company began to dismantle buildings. It wasn't long before nearly all of its residents left town seeking jobs in other mines around the state and beyond. For a number of years Jerome was home to a mere fifty or so people. Buildings sat in disrepair and things looked bleak for this once thriving city. In 1953, a group of concerned citizens formed The Jerome Historical Society and began

---

[1] The year of this publication is 2011. The Bordello may be torn down eventually.

purchasing and restoring unwanted structures mostly in the downtown area. The society has been preserving the rich and sometimes violent history of Jerome ever since. In 1976 Jerome was designated a national historic landmark.

One of the buildings that the Jerome Historical Society saved and in fact now occupies is the old Christ Episcopal Church. This church, constructed in 1927 is now the safe-haven for most of the town's archives. There is very little parking for vehicles on that level of town, so to get there, one must hike up several flights of narrow, uneven concrete steps. It is quite a climb taking into account that the altitude in Jerome is over five-thousand feet.

Once I reached the society, the archivist was very helpful. I was shown an album containing a small handful of pictures of the bordello. No one, however, seemed to know much about the woman who called herself The Cuban Queen. Rumor had it that she was Cuban, Creole, or possibly Mexican and had married a local miner leaving Jerome in the early 1930s. The archives revealed nothing more. They had no photos of the madam nor were they even sure of her real name or ancestry. We spoke for a while, but I never uttered a word about the ghostly woman I had encountered at the property that November day.

Nevertheless, my growing obsession to find out all I could about The Cuban Queen remained undeterred. I began to ask some of the local shop owners and a few of the old-timers for any information they might have about the madam who called herself The Cuban Queen. Unfortunately, even the old-timers were too young to recall any information from the 1920s.

I continued my pursuit, asking questions of anyone who might have had family ties to Jerome. My luck seemed to change when I met an old Mexican man who was well into his eighties. His last name was Sandoval. Sandoval, now living in California, had returned to Arizona for a family reunion. He was born and raised in Jerome and knew a lot about the history of the town. He was an interesting fellow and seemed eager to talk about his old stomping grounds. His father worked in the miles of tunnels underneath the town and died of a heart attack in 1952, four months after copper mining shut down for the last time.

"My father never missed a day of work until they closed down the mine, Sandoval said. *He worked himself to death for the mining company. He had lung trouble, something the doctor called silicosis. He was only forty-eight when he died. After my father died, my mother was never the same. A few of the families stayed around Jerome for a while, they kept hoping the mine would reopen, but it never did. All of the poor widowed women had no other place to go. Some stayed here in Jerome for years selling tamales, or did whatever they could just to survive. Over the years, people gave up and had to move on to find work. My family moved to California in the late 50's when I was in high school."*

As our conversation continued, I asked Mr. Sandoval if he knew anything about the historic Cuban Queen building in the red-light district or of the woman who ran it. He laughed aloud and said, *"Not personally."* Mr. Sandoval did however tell me about a tragic incident that happened at his parents' wedding back in the early 1920's. The event seemed to have a small connection to the Cuban Queen.

According to Sandoval's story, two men got into a gunfight after leaving his parents wedding celebration. A friend of his parents was shot and killed in that fight and a few years later the man's wife was also murdered. Sandoval heard the wife was possibly a prostitute and was apparently shot to death by an estranged lover at The Cuban Queen Bordello. He thought the last name of the two people killed might have been *Villalpando*. He couldn't remember exactly how the story went and didn't really know any of the details, but suggested that perhaps the local newspaper at the time would have reported on the tragedy. As he recalled, his parents were married in 1924.

The next day, I went back to the historical society to look through the old Verde Copper Newspaper articles. I was now looking for anything in the 1920s containing the name "Villalpando". I thought this might have been the Cuban Queen's last name. After some extensive reading and research, I found some very interesting letters written by a family looking for their baby brother with the name of Enrique Villalpando. The boy was about three years old when he was reported missing from Jerome. His family never heard from him again.

The family had tried to locate their missing relative many times without success. They had located the baby boy's baptismal records from the Holy Family Parish in Jerome and had obtained copies of the newspaper articles reporting the tragic murder of their mother Guadalupe (Apadaco) Villalpando and the reporting of the killing of their father Francisco Villalpando.

In one of the letters that I found, the family was asking for information about the woman who owned The Cuban Queen Bordello. They hoped she might shed some light on what happened to their little brother Enrique, but apparently, they gave up their investigation without ever finding him.

At the bottom of the baptismal record were two signatures. One of the signatures, as I found out later, was that of The Cuban Queen herself. She was using one of her many assumed names, *Anita Gonzales* or *Juanita Gonzales*. The family had no way of knowing at the time, but the information they were looking for was right there on the baptismal record.

Following, is a facsimile of Angelina Parra's (Enrique Villalpando's sister) hand written letter to the Jerome Archivist Nancy Smith, requesting the newspaper articles. The family made many inquires, including several visits to Jerome, Arizona in an effort to locate their missing baby brother, Enrique Villalpando,

send me 4 copies of Dad &
mom write-up. I am
referring to the paper article.
My father Francisco
Villalpando & Mother Guadalupe
Apodaca. I am pretty sure
you remember. It was my
brother Raul & Angelina. I am
sending you a copy of my
brother (Enrique Villalpando)
Baptism Certificate. In case
you hear or are able
to inquiry in some way
about something else. I

(over)

I am sending you a money order. Hoping to cover your trouble + postage. Even if you told me it was a donation. You use it for the "Jerome Historical Society"

Thank you very, very much.

Truely yours,

Angelina Parra

Dear Archivist,

Thank you very much for the copies of the Verde Copper newspaper articles on the death of both of my parents, my father, Francisco Villalpando in 1924 and my mother Guadalupe (Lupe) Apadaco Villalpando in 1927.

The articles certainly shed some light on that time. However, we are still trying to find out what happened to our little brother, Enrique Villalpando.

He was three or four years old when taken from Jerome. According to the baptism certificate, Enrique was baptized at the Holy Family Parish in Jerome Arizona on December 11, 1924. His birth date on the document is August 3, 1923. My brothers and I were raised by my uncle Apadaco (mom's brother) after she was killed. I have learned from family members that mother worked for a woman who ran a 'House' or a saloon. Are there any records of those kinds of places available? Perhaps that woman left town with our little brother. Any information no matter how small even if it is just hearsay might be helpful in locating him, assuming he is still alive. Will you please put out a request to the old-timers of Jerome for any information they might have heard or know? I'm a sending a money order hoping to cover your trouble and postage.

I sincerely appreciate all your help.

Thank you for all your time.

Yours truly, Angelina Parra

Above is a facsimile of a typed letter, thanking the archivist for the newspaper articles.

This is a facsimile of Enrique Villalpando's Baptism Certificate.

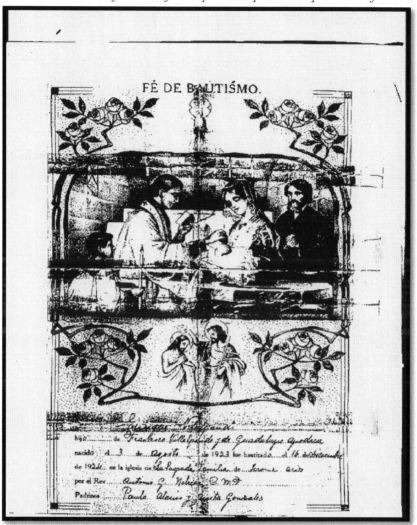

Anita Gonzales's signature is on the bottom of Enrique Villalpando's Baptism Certificate

After extensive research, I was able to uncover some family history and expose the true identity of the woman who called herself Anita Gonzales, Juanita Gonzales and even Annie Johnson. I discovered they were all the same person; namely, the one and only Cuban Queen herself.

The events presented here are as close to the facts as I could obtain. For the purpose of this account and to eliminate confusion, I will repeatedly refer to this woman as "The Queen" or "The Cuban Queen".

A photo of the Holy Family Parish Jerome Arizona, where Enrique Villalpando was baptized in 1924.

Chapter 3

The Cuban Queen is Born

She was born on Friday the 13th

The Cuban Queen was born into this world on Friday the 13th of April, 1883, as **Bessie Julia Johnson**. She used many assumed names over her lifetime. Some of the names included Bessie Seymour, Julia Johnson, Juanita Gonzales, Anita Gonzales, Anita Morton, Annie Johnson, Anita Ford and The Cuban Queen.

Her family's history began in the 1800s with her grandmother, Julia Jenkins. Julia was a slave on a Mississippi cotton plantation and used the surname of her master, J. C. Jenkins. In 1860, J. C. Jenkins was one of the largest slaveholders in the South. He held as many as 523 slaves in Adams County, Mississippi. The Queen's grandmother, Julia, worked as a cook in his home, commonly referred to as the *big house*. The cooks ordered all of the food and made all of the meals for the master's family. House slaves held a higher status than field slaves did. Most house slaves had better clothing and improved cottages that were located closer to the big house. These slaves were usually house cleaners, servants and cooks. Most slaves were not permitted to learn to read or write. If they were caught studying, they could be punished by law. The lawbreaker, at the discretion of any justice of the peace, could receive harsh punishment – up to twenty lashes for each offense. Occasionally, a house slave would secretly learn to read by hearing others read aloud, or by becoming friends with the master's children who then taught them behind closed doors.

Enslaved women were often forced to submit to the brutal sexual desires of their masters. This sexual abuse ranged from sexual coercion from plantation owners, to forced breeding with other slave men for the sole purpose of reproducing more slaves for profit.

It wasn't uncommon for a white slave master to take a young female virgin slave at the age of twelve or thirteen and force her to submit to his sexual wishes. This, of course, sometimes resulted in pregnancy.

The Queen's grandmother was thought to have been a victim of sexual abuse by her master, J. C. Jenkins and consequently became pregnant. She was only fourteen when she gave birth to a baby girl. She named her daughter Hattie Jenkins. The Queen's mother Hattie was born into slavery on October 4, 1858 and was labeled a *mulatto*, which is a person of half African or Negro ancestry and half European or White ancestry. Being the offspring of Master Jenkins, Hattie was given a few more privileges than some of the other slaves, but nonetheless was still a slave.

The terms *mulatto* and *octoroon* originated with the racial policies of European colonizers in the Americas, especially when the civil rights and responsibilities were based directly on the degree of European blood a person possessed. These classifications were carefully recorded. While these terms have highly precise definitions, in actual practice they were often used on impressions of skin color rather than definite knowledge of ancestry.

Hattie Jenkins was seven years old when the United States Constitution's Thirteenth Amendment was adopted and slavery was officially abolished. Hattie grew up quickly and became quite an enterprising woman. At various times in her life she worked as a cook, a laundress, a harlot, a saloonkeeper and a mortician's assistant. At the young age of fourteen, Hattie had her first child, a boy she named William White, sometimes called Bill or Willie. William's father was a European man named Grandville White. Grandville White was a former slave owner and later became the postmaster in Bullock County, Alabama. Hattie's second child was also a boy. She named him Robert. Robert's father was a black man, but his name is unknown. Her third child was a girl she named **Bessie Julia Johnson.** Somewhere around the time Bessie was born, her mother Hattie Jenkins married a black man named Richard Johnson. It is not known, however, whether Mr. Johnson was indeed Bessie's biological father. Bessie's skin color was lighter, the color of an *octoroon*. Bessie Johnson was born on Friday, April 13th in 1883 in Montgomery, Alabama. Hattie and Mr. Johnson lived together only a few short years. During that time, Hattie had her fourth child. They named him James (Bookie) Johnson.

In 1887, Hattie and her four children moved from Alabama to New Orleans. In the years to follow, Hattie had three more children, Martin, David, and Ollie (or Dink) as he was called. Their father was a black man thought to be named Duplain W. Rhodes.

Mr. Rhodes was in the business of hauling things for people. His business soon developed into transporting the deceased to their awaiting gravesite. Mr. Rhodes later decided to go into the funeral business to provide burial services for the Negros of New Orleans. He soon owned and operated the city's first undertaking business. He established his first funeral home on Valence Street in uptown New Orleans. In spite of having some of the finest horses around, Mr. Rhodes soon realized the advantages of using a motorized vehicle for his business. In 1917, he was reportedly the first Black person in New Orleans to own an automobile.

Fast forward: in 2005, one of the most catastrophic natural disasters in our nation's history, Hurricane Katrina, ravaged Southeast Louisiana and the Gulf Coast. The storm devastated the Rhodes's property. The roof was blown off and the property filled with water. Coffins were floating about and everything was destroyed. The Rhodes family rebuilt, and the Rhodes Funeral Home in New Orleans is still in business today 125 years later!

While in New Orleans, the Johnson family became close friends with a boy in the neighborhood. His name was Ferddy Mouton. As a young boy, Ferddy was infatuated with Dink's older sister, Bessie. He thought she was the prettiest girl he had ever seen. Bessie was eight years older than Ferddy, and at the time, she had no interest in her brother's little friend. Later in her life, however, that would all change.

The Johnson brothers and Ferddy Mouton played for pennies in little groups called *spasm bands*. They also joined in the marching bands that followed the funeral processions. Just about anyone was welcome to contribute as long as they could beat a drum or blow a horn. Being so young at the time, the boys weren't exactly playing tubas and bass drums, but simply contributing to the band with homemade instruments illustrating their driving interest in music. These interests would flourish in the years to come.

In the 1890s, it was customary in New Orleans to commemorate a death with a *funeral feast* celebrating with an abundance of food and music. Music would set the mood of the occasion and a slow march to the graveyard would follow.

Hattie Johnson and her family lived with the undertaker for approximately five years. During that time, Hattie helped prepare and lay out the bodies of the dead. She quickly learned that not all deaths were just an act of nature. Many black people died of suicide, hanging, drowning, murder and poisoning. Others died of typhoid fever, malaria and pneumonia. The deceased had to be cared for and transported to the gravesite swiftly so as not to spread disease. At the time, blacks were not permitted in the white people's mortuary, so most often they were prepared in the horse stables. Most funerals used horse and wagon to carry the dead to the cemetery, but the poor would use handcarts. There was also a lack of cold storage in the 1890's, which was another obvious reason to deal rapidly with the dead. Coins or stones were placed on the eyes to keep them from opening and a bandage was tied under the chin to the top of the head to hold the jaw closed. Ropes were also used to tie down the limbs. This kept them in place before *rigor mortis* set in.

Wood handcart used to transport bodies to gravesite

By the early age of ten years, Bessie was already well aware of the grim details of death. It must have been a bizarre life, especially for a child, to live and work with the undertaker. It is hard to know what ill effects it may have had on such a young girl as she was growing up. Bessie was the only girl among her six brothers. She was a pretty child, a bit spoiled and was quite used to getting her own way. She grew into an exceptionally beautiful young woman with a figure most girls would sell their souls for.

Name (Sex Race)	Relationship	Born	Occupation
Hattie Johnson (F M)	Head	October 1860	Laundress
Willie Johnson (M M)	Son	August 1876	Musician
Robert Johnson (M B)	Son	November 1880	At School
Bessie Johnson (FM)	Daughter	April 1883	At School
James Johnson (M B)	Son	September 1887	At School
David Johnson (M B)	Son	October 1890	-
Ollie Johnson (M B)	Son	January 1892	-
(U.S. Census 1900, Mississippi, Harrison County, Biloxi, Beat 1, SD6 ED23, Sheet 9A, Lines 2-8, household at Deloney Street, Biloxi)			

1900 US Census, for Hattie Johnson's household Harrison County,

9A Deloney St. Biloxi, Mississippi

Hattie, Bill and Bessie's race is marked with an 'M' for Mulatto. The rest of the family is marked with a 'B' for Black.

Sex - (M Male   (F) Female

Race - (W) White   (B) Black   (M) Mulatto

The Johnson family was now comprised of seven children by at least four different fathers. The entire family kept the last name Johnson. It may have been that Mr. Johnson was the only man, which Hattie legally married.

The 1900 census from Harrison County, Biloxi, Mississippi, does raise a question or two. The census does not mention a husband in the household. It appears Hattie Johnson was raising her children on her own as *head of household*. It seems the family was no longer living with Mr. Rhodes, the undertaker.

Bessie grew up fast and followed close in her mother's footsteps. As a result, she became pregnant at the early age of sixteen. The father of the baby was a French Creole man named Fred Seymour. He was the proprietor of a local saloon. It is not known if Fred Seymour and Bessie Johnson were ever legally married or simply lived together in a common-law relationship. Whatever the case, she gave birth to a daughter and named her Hattie Julia Seymour after her mother and grandmother. Fred's and Bessie's relationship did not last long. Shortly after the break-up, her restless spirit spoke, and she left her baby daughter with her mother, Hattie and moved on.

In 1902, Bessie decided to go visit her older brother, Bill Johnson, and look for work. Bill was a very successful musician living and working in New Orleans. He started his career as a guitarist, but later became quite accomplished at the upright bass. Bill was working at The Mahogany Hall on Basin Street for the famous Storyville Madam, Lulu White. Bill Johnson, made famous a move called the *syncopated, single–stroke hook*. This meant, hooking the right index finger under the bass string, pulling it outward and letting it snap back against the fingerboard.

Bill worked in New Orleans as early as the 1890s playing with groups like the *Peerless Band* and the *Eagle Band*. In 1907, Bill left New Orleans and went to California where he formed one of the first jazz bands known as *The Original Creole Orchestra*. The band was a big success and toured the country on the *Orpheum* circuit. Bill Johnson became one of the greatest bass players who ever lived and contributed much to the early jazz sound. Bill lived to be over 100 years old. He died in Texas in 1976.

The Original Creole Orchestra
c. 1908-1918 Bill Johnson (upper right)

Bessie's youngest brother, Dink Johnson also played in Bill's Original Creole Orchestra. Noted as one of the best drummers of his time, Dink worked as both a drummer and a piano player all over Mississippi and in New Orleans before moving to the western United States. In 1914, Dink moved to the frontier town of Las Vegas, Nevada where he played the piano and helped manage the *Arcade Saloon*.

In the 1920's, Dink led a band in California called the *Five Hounds of Jazz*. The band was later renamed the *Los Angeles Six*. He made his first recording on the clarinet in 1922 with *Kid Ory's Original Creole Jazz Band* on the Sunshine label. He also recorded for several other labels and was one of the first musicians to record *One Man Band* music where he would play the piano, the drums and the clarinet, recording them together using a technique known as *over-dubbing*.

Later in life, Dink ran his own restaurant called *Dink's Place* located at 4229 Avalon Boulevard in Los Angeles. Dink's Place, although not nationally known, was quite the nightspot for the locals. Patrons could listen to him perform on a nightly basis. Sadly, the luster of Dink Johnson's milestone faded. He became an alcoholic and a slave to the bottle. He eventually drank himself to death, a seemingly common demise for entertainers. Dink Johnson died in Portland, Oregon, in 1954 at the age of 62.

Like her musician brothers, Bessie (The Queen), was also in the entertainment business. Her profession of choice however, was prostitution. It was difficult for a woman in the 1800s to earn a significant amount of honest money, so The Queen did what she knew best. She was determined to get her piece of the money pie, so she quickly found work in the red-light district of New Orleans called *Storyville*.

She started by taking back her maiden name, Johnson and used her middle name Julia as her first name. The new Julia Johnson became a first class *sporting woman,* working for Madam Antonia Gonzalez. Julia quickly learned that you had to hustle to advance, and she did just that. Not only did she charge for sexual favors, but she also became first-rate at hustling drinks and selling dances. It was standard for sporting women to keep 40% of their fee and pay the balance to their *landlords*. She became quite a hustler and when it came to integrity versus money, money would win every time. Often she would receive lavish gratuities in many forms such as cash, jewelry, furs and even diamonds. Some said she was also known to occasionally fleece her clients. To say the least, Julia did very well as a *sporting woman* in Storyville.

Storyville was located just behind the French Quarter and covered sixteen square blocks. When a gentleman would step off the train in New Orleans, he was given a little blue book. The book contained the addresses and descriptions of all the local houses of ill repute.

These detailed books were guides to the district's services including house descriptions, particular services, prices and the type of "stock" each house had to offer. Sex was always the lure of the Storyville district, and music always seemed to set the tempo.

Chapter 4

The Story of Storyville

Basin Street brothels in Storyville, New Orleans c. 1900s

Storyville was the legalized prostitution district of New Orleans from 1897 to 1917. After many public protests concerning the widespread prostitution in New Orleans, a law was enacted limiting brothels, saloons, and other businesses of vice to a single sixteen-block area. The new district was named after Alderman Sydney Story, the author of the legislation. The first brothel on the right in the above photo at 235 Basin Street was Lulu White's.

Next, in the small older building was Martha Clarke's. The building with the rounded cupola was Josie Arlington's and then next-door was Hilma Burts' place. A little further down the block was Countess Willie Piazza's Villa. In this high-rent section of Storyville on Basin Street, every nightspot also had its own brand of music. The madams of these red-light establishments hired mainly black musicians to entertain the customers in their brothels and saloons. The area was two blocks inland from the French Quarter and included sixteen square blocks from Iberville to Saint Louis Street, and Robertson to Basin Street. It was one of the city's largest attractions.

At the top of the ladder was Tom Anderson, a white man and the self-proclaimed mayor of Storyville. Second in command were the richest white madams whose names and fame were widespread. Equally noted were their sizeable establishments. There was Gypsy Shafer, Mud Tuckerman, Emma Johnson and Miss Hilma Burts, just to name a few. Next in command were madams regarded as people of color including the famous Lulu White, (*Octoroon*), Antonia Gonzalez (*Hispanic*) and Willie Piazza, (*Italian*) Willie held her nightly get-togethers in a luxurious Italian-style villa.

Madam Gonzalez's house, sat on a stone foundation a few feet higher than the street level. Five red brick steps lead to the door at the main entrance. On the glass portion of the door, the inscription read, *Gonzalez, Female Cornetist.*

Antonia Gonzalez advertised herself as the only madam to play the cornet naked. The place was not a posh mansion for the rich out-of-town visitors, but it was a popular place and well respected in the community.

An advertisement in the *Blue Book* for Miss Antonia Gonzalez read: *For ragtime, singing, stimulating dancing and fun in general, Miss Antonia P. Gonzalez stands in a class alone. We are two doors up from the corner of Villere and Bienville Street. Any person out for fun among the first-class Octoroons or pretty Creole damsels, call 1974. Remember the phone number, 1974.*

Bessie Julia Johnson (The Queen) was twenty years old when she began work as a *sporting lady*. She was one of eight girls working for Madam Antonia Gonzalez and Gipsy Shafer. This brothel was said to have specialized in particularly lewd exhibitions.

Storyville bestowed sexual privileges on white males only. Black males were barred from purchasing services in either black or white brothels. This to some, was an offensive double standard, but nonetheless, was the law in Storyville. The women who identified themselves as octoroons for the purpose of sexual commerce, placed themselves above the darker skinned prostitutes and promoted themselves as the "best of both worlds". This offered wealthy white men in pursuit of sexual pleasures a chance to transgress the color lines. Women were listed in the Blue Book by both race, and in alphabetical order.

The Queen's full name was Bessie Julia Johnson, and it is believed she was listed in the Blue Book under her middle name, Julia. A Julia Johnson appeared in the colored section under the letter 'J' in the Blue Book's 1906 edition. Often, sporting women would use their middle names or even an entirely fabricated name, so as not to embarrass their families. The Blue Books were small, approximately four to five inches so they would easily tuck into a man's pocket. They were distributed at places like train stations, bars and barbershops.

LETTER "I" (COLORED)

Ingram, Delia	1524 Bienville
Irwin, Lotta	1501 Conti

LETTER "J" (COLORED)

Jordan, Ida	1511 Customhouse
Jefferson, Mary	1522 Customhouse
Jacobs, Alice	1567 Customhouse
Jackson, Henrietta	1427 Bienville
Johnson, Rosie	1422 Bienville
Jones, Lottie	1424 Bienville
Jones, Ella	1426 Bienville
Johnson, Julia	1540 Bienville
Jones, Georgie	1525 Conti
Jackkson, Antonia	1549 Conti
Johnson, Annie	1563 Conti
Johnson, Lulu	1408 St. Louis
Jackson, Mary	228 N. Robertson
Johnson, Eleonora	229 N. Villere
Johnston, Emma	322 N. Marais
Jackson, Lulu	208 N. Liberty
Jackson, Glydes	223 N. Liberty
Jones, Bettie	333 N. Liberty
James, Beatrice	337 N. Liberty
Jones, Martha	405 N. Liberty
Johnson, Willie	330 N. Marais

A page from the 1906 Blue Book in the colored section under 'J'
Her tagline read; *You might forget my name, but you'll never forget my figure.*

The publication also advertised various other products and services such as taxi rides, cigars, liquor and other forms of entertainment. The Blue Book served as a directory for over 700 prostitutes. It gave their names, addresses and type of services offered. Some girls chose to be a bit more descriptive than others. The book contained only the women who worked in the finer sporting houses. There were no listings for common streetwalkers or prostitutes found in the numerous *cribs*. Most of these types of prostitutes would service any filthy, drunken man and do just about anything for a few cents.

The Queen, now known as Julia Johnson, was always well dressed, sexy and shrewd. She became quite skilled at her profession. She demanded a high price and was sought after by many. Julia advertised herself as a pretty, light-skinned, first class Octoroon. The higher-class sporting women kept business cards on hand and distributed them whenever an opportunity arose. The Queen's employer, Miss Antonia Gonzalez, was located in the section of Storyville called The Camel Backs. The name *Camel Back* was derived from an architectural perspective of sorts. It portrayed those houses that had one or two stories in the front and two or three stories in the rear. The streets in this area were roughly paved with cobblestones. There was no modern sewer system, and as a result, scum and sewage from the chamber pots would often be standing in the gutters. The pungent smell of ammonia constantly lingered in the heavy New Orleans air.

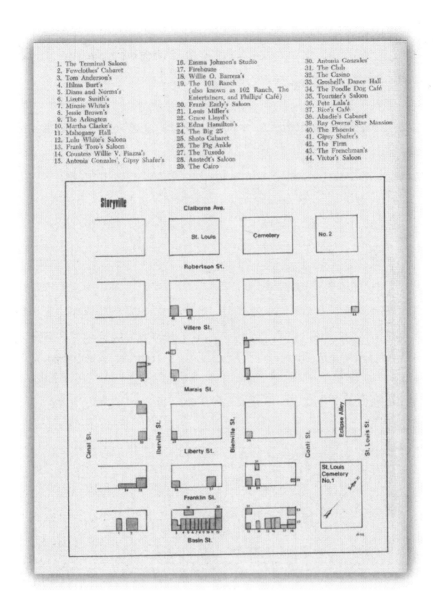

A page form a Blue Book 1897-1925
Lot #15, Basin St. & Bienville St. was Antonia Gonzales's & Gipsy Shafer's
The Queen aka, *Julia Johnson's* address was 1540 Bienville.

Inside the seemingly plush establishments, ornate tapestries and paintings seemed to be the method of covering holes in the walls and floors. Silverfish, cockroaches and mice were everywhere. The sight in the back alleys was even more revolting. There were piles of rotting garbage, sewage, and the decaying remains of butchered animals scattered about. Rats, dogs and cats ran rampant in the streets.

Oddly enough, it was in this section of town called The Camelbacks where the establishments served real food for the local working people. Southern fried chicken, red beans and rice, gumbo, and crab cakes were among the favorites. This is where the locals gathered to meet and eat. It was not a glitzy or festive neighborhood. The dance halls and flashy places were two or three blocks toward the river.

Farther up the block from Gonzalez's, on the corner of Bienville Street and Villere Street, was another place called *The Frenchman's*. This was a fabulous place for many locals to party after they finished their nights work. Actors, performers, and musicians would come to The Frenchman's to listen and learn from the best. Musicians like Tony Jackson, Kid Ory, King Oliver, Buddy Bolden, Bill Johnson, and Ferddy Mouton would come and share their talent with each other. Ferddy Mouton, The Queen's friend was one of the district's well-known *piano professors*. Ferddy played piano for just about every brothel at one time or another. The Frenchman's was a place where all the boys with nimble fingers would get into a battle of the pianos, and their weapons were their notes. It was in this dark, smoky backroom at The Frenchman's that jazz was born. Jazz was woven from many different styles of music. It was blues, stomp, ragtime, swing and spirituals all wrapped into one. Occasionally, the after-hours parties at The Frenchman's would continue well into the next day. If the liquor supply at the bar was not enough to keep the party going all night, the patrons would walk across the street and pick up something from the twenty-four hour drugstore. *Crown*, a powder form of cocaine, could be purchased over the counter and marijuana cigarettes were sold for just five cents each.

In some ways, this twenty-four-hour city called Storyville was much like Las Vegas, Nevada is today. The actors and entertainers would go to bed sometime in the late morning hours. Meanwhile, the shy people with thin smiles were in their respective kitchens baking bread and washing dirty dishes. The seemingly invisible janitors and housekeepers were mopping up the sticky spills and dumping overflowing ashtrays from the night before. The smell of stale beer mixed with disinfectants permeated the air. In the daylight, nothing looked the same as the night before. The bright midday sunlight seemed to expose the many imperfections of these structures, both inside and out. Evidence of numerous concealed transgressions of the night before became all too evident in the daylight hours.

By four in the afternoon, the madams and their sporting ladies sat down to an early dinner and made plans for that night's entertainment. After dinner, everyone would bathe, put on their makeup and dress for the evening's revelry. Before long, the walls would echo with music, chatter and laughter, and once again the smell of wine, whiskey, cigar smoke and cheap perfume choked the air.

The brothels of Storyville became great mansions of vice. Saloon owners pushing their watered-down liquor, politicians with their empty promises, and of course the corrupt law enforcement who took large cuts in bribes, all made out like *fat cats*. Many madams became extraordinarily wealthy as did a few sporting women. Millions of dollars found its way from the stockings and corsets of these sly, cunning prostitutes into the local banks.

Almost every available building was either a bar or a brothel. What these nightspots had in common was liquor, prostitution, music and gambling and most of it was legal. The red-light district called Storyville was a proverbial gold mine, and the sporting ladies were in the center of it all. They served the over-priced drinks, collected the money, danced and entertained the men.

Besides being profitable, this business also, however, had its dark side. While venereal diseases were all too common, an even more frightening scenario for the sporting women was pregnancy. If a sporting woman accidentally became pregnant, she would more than likely lose her job. There were remedies for this, but they were far from pleasant.

Unwanted pregnancies were terminated through a number of techniques. An abortion was referred to as *a cleaning*. Sharpened implements like metal coat hangers, spoons and knitting needles were just some of the tools used to execute this *cleaning* by dilating the cervix and scraping out the inside of the uterus. Another method used was punching or jumping on the stomach creating severe abdominal trauma. Long-term damage or even death sometimes occurred by using these crude methods. Herbal remedies were also used to encourage miscarriages. Teas made from herbs like Sineca, Tansy, Bitter Buttons, Snakeweed, Prickly Cucumber seeds and Black Cohosh were commonly used. One contraceptive that seemed to work well as a vaginal suppository was prepared from raw honeycomb and alligator dung. This birth control method of honey and dung in fact, goes back to ancient times and can be found in ancient Egyptian writings. The alligator dung worked as a spermicide, the honey kept it sticky and the honeycomb melted slowly.

A sporting woman in need of a cleaning would pay dearly for these voodoo techniques and concoctions. Many of these mixtures were kept secret and only known by a Voodoo Witch. Voodoo was more or less the unsanctioned religion of Storyville.

Even though these risky practices often left drastic physical and mental repercussions for the mother and unwanted child, it seemed to some, less criminal to abort the child than to curse it with an unwelcomed existence. Nevertheless, even with all these extra precautions, a sizable number of children were born in the attics of these establishments. Midwives would help with the birth of the baby when a prostitute became pregnant. They called these babies *Parlor* or *Trick Babies*.

Most of the fathers of these illegitimate children were rich *Johns* from out of town and were never aware of the child. Often these children would be physically or mentally handicapped from an attempted abortion or from the alcohol and drug abuse of the mother.

Frequently, the fate of many Storyville sporting women was not a cheerful one. Many women became depressed and dependent on either narcotics or alcohol. Some died horribly from the effects of a venereal disease, and frequently women were found murdered.

An oral story told by Pearl Sue as she recalls her early years in Storyville.

"I think I was twelve and starting to get pubic hair when Mama sold my virginity to an old bald man for twenty dollars and 3 ounces of opium. I was thirteen, nearly fourteen when I started turning tricks on a daily basis.

My Mama was one of them sporting women in Storyville, New Orleans. I was fifteen years old when the authorities found my mom strangled to death in her room.

I was told I was born in the attic of one of those fancy mansions on May 6th, 1901. As far as I know, I never had a birth certificate. Mom said she had no idea who my father might have been.

When I was young, I can remember living in the attic of one of those fancy mansions. There were about eight or nine of us kids up there. A few boys, but mostly girls, some kids had their problems. Some were mental and some were physical.

Us kids lived in a world of our own up there, seldom seen or heard. Our food, mostly leftovers, was brought up to us. We slept on dirty blankets on the floor. We played games, sometimes nasty ones, but we all knew when and where to hide and when to be quiet.

Pearl Sue, c. 1917

One night, I walked in on my mom downstairs. She was with a half-juiced John, and he had his pants down. Mom said to the John, "*It's okay, she's my kid.*" I think I was seven or eight at the time.

Then my mom asked me if I wanted to help her. She gave me a washrag, and I helped her wash the man with this purple stuff. The man gave me a quarter, and that is how it started.

The Johns never bothered me much. I was too young to even have a shape back then.

I would get money to help my mom with the Johns. There would always be a quarter or two in it for me. I spent most my money on hard candy.

Some of the other younger girls and sometimes the boys did the same. It went over big with the Johns. Sometimes the sporting ladies used us kids in their acts.

All of us kids were well aware of what was going on. The young girls were expected to follow in their mother's footsteps. But for the young boys, it was a different story. They were just lost to society, no one wanted the boys.

They had to fend for themselves, stealing what they could and eating out of garbage cans just to survive. Most had no education, no jobs and no place to go.

Many of the young boys lived, fought and died on the streets of Storyville, New Orleans and no one seemed to care".

Yours truly, Pearl Sue

A Gentleman From Storyville Reported:

Those sporting places were trained to take every last cent you had. After a couple of strong over-priced drinks, you would be a little loose with your money. A clever well-dressed woman would drag you out on the dance floor. As you dance, she would be rubbing up to you. She would be whispering in your ear, telling you how handsome you were, and how good she could make you feel, and how bad she wanted you. Once you were upstairs with her, she would offer extras for another price. It was hard to resist. After you were in her room and the door closed, the process took about five minutes. Next thing you knew, you would be standing alone in the hallway outside her room half dressed without a cent in your pocket and no place to go but home. The party was over, and she had all of your money. Of course, the women never tried to sell you anything afterward. These women were smart enough to know the man leaving was not the same man as the man entering. In a matter of minutes, your woman would be all dressed and downstairs sizing up her next victim.

In the few years that followed, Storyville became a very dangerous place. Venereal disease was running rampant and robberies and murders were occurring daily. For a few women, including The Queen, the experience as a sporting woman was a gold mine. The Queen left Storyville in 1908 taking with her a sizeable bankroll. She had always aspired to go into business for herself and now she had both the money and the practical knowledge to do just that. It wouldn't be long before she would find herself as the madam of her own thriving business in another city.

In 1917 by order of the Secretary of the Navy, Storyville came to a screeching halt. The Secretary claimed that more than half of his young Navy boys had a venereal disease, and many of his men had been beaten, robbed and even murdered. Storyville became a ghost town almost overnight. The old red-light district of New Orleans that once boasted of fancy sporting places with elaborate decor, musical entertainment and a wide variety of working women, was now history. Gone were the women in the cribs and back alleys. Gone were the celebrated madams and pretty sporting ladies. Everything they owned was piled into handcarts and pushed away by old men or young boys. Gone were the flamboyant piano professors. The only things that remained were several heavy out-of-tune pianos. Their once highly polished mahogany wood and sparkling ebony and ivory keys, were now covered in a ghostly dust speckled with mouse droppings.

A District filled with greed, excitement, sin and the sound of jazz became just a memory. The music invented in Storyville, however would live on. American jazz music would spread quickly across the country, and following closely behind were, of course, the *Jazzebells.* Jazzebell was the new word for the whores who followed the jazz musicians as they played their gigs around the country.

One of the most famous among these traveling musicians was a jazz piano player, a Creole man named Ferddy Mouton.

Chapter 5

Mr. Piano Man

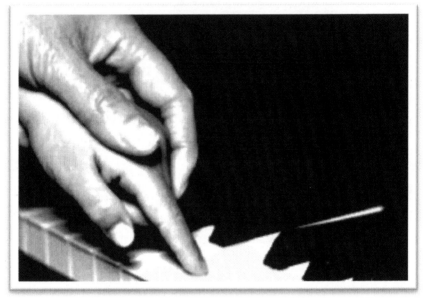

Ferddy started playing the piano at an early age.

Ferddy Mouton was born in Gulfport, Louisiana, on Oct 20, 1890. His given name was Ferdinand Joseph LaMothe. Ferddy's parents were both American citizens from New Orleans, Louisiana. Ferddy's mother, Louise Monette, was a mix of African and French descent, commonly known as *Louisiana Creole*, and she was a *free person of color.*

His father, Edward J. LaMothe, was of Haitian ancestry and employed by the U.S. Naval Intelligent Service. He often traveled to both Haiti and Santo Domingo in pursuance of his duties for the U.S. Government.

Mr. LaMothe was a classically schooled trombonist with formal musical training and could read and write music as well as play by ear. He started teaching his young son, Ferddy to play piano at a very young age. He often took Ferddy to the French Opera in New Orleans and exposed him to fine music.

Ferddy's father and mother separated when he was four or five years old and Ferddy remained with his mother, Louise in New Orleans. His mother soon remarried a man named Willie Mouton and Ferddy then inherited his stepfather's last name. Each summer, Ferddy would stay with his Godmother Eulalie, or *Echo,* as they called her. She owned a farm in Biloxi, Mississippi, and raised strawberries in the summertime. Echo was a distant relative on his father's side of the family and spoke only a language called *Haitian Creole French.* Ferddy could speak some Creole, so there was never any problem communicating. Echo was particularly fond of young Ferddy. She recognized the young boy's talent and paid for piano lessons when he was just six years old.

Ferddy, like his father, had an excellent ear for music and learned quickly. At the age of nine, Ferddy was playing guitar, juice harp, harmonica and piano. By the time he was a young teenager, he had also learned to play most of the brass instruments. Soon, Ferddy could play just about anything he put his hands on. His favorite and most accomplished instrument though, was the piano. His dream at a young age was to become a famed pianist. He enjoyed classical music and opera, but he preferred the more popular types of music, like Ragtime, Latin and Blues. Of course, he also learned the traditional New Orleans music from the streets. Ferddy's mother, Louise, died when he was just fourteen years old. He then lived with his Grandmother Laura Monette.

Ferddy then found himself torn between two worlds. There was his Grandma Laura on his mother's side, who wanted to raise him Catholic and banned him from playing what she called "that dirty devil music" in their home. The other world was his Godmother Echo's on his father's side. Echo believed in voodoo incantations and the underworld and encouraged him to play in the sporting houses of the red-light district. She simply told him, "That's where the money is."

Ultimately, Ferddy chose the underworld. By the time he was fifteen, he was making respectable money playing the piano for tips in the red-light district known as Storyville. Always needing to look good, Ferddy spent most of what he made on fancy clothes.

When his Grandmother Laura found out where the money was coming from, she thought Ferddy had surely sold his soul to the devil. Concerned that he might corrupt the morals of his younger siblings, she disowned him for

"playing that devils music in those wicked places", and no longer allowed him to live in her home. Now, with his mother passed on, and his Grandma Laura refusing to let him live with her, Ferddy was not only a motherless boy, but also homeless. This traumatic event left fifteen-year-old Ferddy emotionally devastated. He walked the streets of New Orleans for days trying to figure out what to do.

Ferddy was an extremely thin boy and was not well suited for hard physical labor. He tried his hand at few jobs here and there, but no matter what he did or where he went he just couldn't get those pounding rhythms and the sound of that music and out of his head.

Dejected and confused, Ferddy decided to hop on a train to Biloxi, Mississippi, and ask his Godmother Echo for advice. Echo encouraged him to continue pursuing his music and said she would perform a ritual to ensure his success. Ferddy always claimed she was a voodoo priestess of some sort, and that she made a lot of money practicing *Black Magic*. In addition, Ferddy was told that there was a family bloodline connection between his godmother and the famed and unchallenged *Queen of Voodoo, Marie Laveau*. Both Marie Laveau and Echo's ancestors were from Santo Domingo. Voodoo is said to be a powerful and mystical practice that can bring spectacular gifts and rewards to those who believe. It goes hand-in-hand with jazz music, Cajun food and Mardi Gras. This mystical religion was and still is a big part of the New Orleans culture.

Ferddy said, *"Very prominent people would consult my Godmother Echo for help. She would look into her crystal ball and tell them their future. Depending on their problem, she would mix up some herbs or other concoction. Sometimes she would give them uncooked turtle heart, black cat bones or gofer,* (graveyard dust). *Other times she would give them colored stones or make them a voodoo doll. If someone wanted to end a relationship, she told them to give that person a **black rose** made from paper, feathers or black silk. Giving a black rose was a symbol for moving on, a fare-thee-well, or the end or death of a relationship or situation."*

Ferddy always believed that his Godmother Echo made a deal with Satan, and that his soul was the ransom for his musical talent. Ferddy said, *"Before you can become a voodoo witch, you have to sell the soul of person you love the very most to Satan as a sacrifice. My godmother, Echo, loved me that much."*

With renewed courage from his godmother, Ferddy promptly made up his mind to go back to New Orleans. He would make his fortune as a piano player in the sporting houses of Storyville. The first thing he did was change his last name from Mouton to Morton. Ferddy said he didn't want to use the French last name of his stepfather for fear of being called *Frenchy*. Once the new Ferddy Morton began playing in the sporting houses, he became quite thrilled with not only the money he was making, but also the constant female attention he was receiving. It wasn't long before Ferddy adopted a certain high and mighty, egotistical attitude that would later become one of his many trademarks.

While still in his teens, Ferddy Morton became the *piano professor* for the famous Madam Hilma Burts in her large Storyville mansion of vice called *The Mirror Ballroom*. This brothel became well noted for a performance called *The Naked Dance*. When the Naked Dance was called, Ferddy would pull out one of his fast-tempo numbers. A beautiful woman would enter the room and dance naked on the table tops, spinning faster and faster to the music. Ferddy always said the Naked Dance was quite an art form. It later became the title to one of Ferddy's more famous compositions.

Young Ferddy is playing the piano with his back to the crowd. Hilma Burts is the madam sitting right of the piano with sporting girls on the left. C. early 1900's.

It was 1905 and Ferddy was now making over a hundred dollars a night playing the piano in the Mirror Ballroom. By the end of his stay in New Orleans, Ferddy Morton had played piano for just about every sporting house in Storyville. Around 1907, he left New Orleans and for the next twenty years went on the road playing virtually every nightclub that existed. He also spent time traveling with various vaudeville and minstrel shows, which took him to almost every state in the USA. Ferddy was not only a talented musician, but he would also work in a variety of acts showing his flair as a comedian and a dancer.

Vaudeville *(voix de ville or voice of the city)* shows were the most popular entertainment form in America in the early 1900's. The shows were reasonably priced and attracted a diverse audience. White performers would cover their faces with burnt cork, a style of make-up commonly known as *blackface.*

Vaudeville performers would mimic the *down on the farm* lifestyle of the uneducated slaves. Although this type of entertainment today would certainly be considered racially

humiliating, it was quite popular with the audiences at the time. The vaudeville shows reached the peak of their success in 1910 with silent films on the horizon.

Eager to learn, Ferddy traveled to the gulf coast and southern states picking up tips from other musicians. This helped shape Ferddy's style of music, which in turn, molded him into nothing short of a musical genius. Ferddy often played the melody of a song with his right thumb while playing harmony above these notes with his other fingers on his right hand. He walked major and minor sixths in the bass with a basic swing rhythm with his left hand and played diminished fifth notes above the melody with his right hand instead of tenths or octaves giving his music an unforgettable out-of-tune sound. This style and resonance continues to be recognized today as "New Orleans Jazz".

Ferddy had become not only a dazzling showman with a wardrobe to match, but he had also become a king in the underworld. Smoking a big cigar and packing a pearl handled pistol, he had transformed himself from a skinny homeless and motherless French Creole boy, into a smooth talking, big shot piano man. Ferddy Morton was an extremely colorful character and methodically generated his own publicity, doing so mostly by bragging.

Meanwhile, in 1912, The Queen's older brother, Bill Johnson was forming a jazz band called *The Original Creole Orchestra*. Her little brother Dink was the band's drummer for a while, but later moved to Las Vegas with her. The Queen was, in part, the financial backer for the band. Bill still needed a good piano player, so he invited their old friend, Ferddy, from New Orleans to come to Los Angeles and sit in with the band. Ferddy accepted, and soon the band became a big success. They toured around the country for several years. By 1917, The Original Creole Orchestra was breaking up and the members went off in different directions. Bill went off to Chicago and found himself playing at the *Royal Gardens*.

When the piano professor (Ferddy Morton) got wind of how well The Queen's new Las Vegas business was doing, he thought he might like a piece of the Las Vegas action himself. He decided to take a train trip from Los Angeles to Las Vegas and see his old girlfriend Bessie, (The Queen), and her brother, Dink Johnson. Ferddy was excited to check out the new frontier town and hoped to do a little gambling and maybe even play some music there. It was Feb. 10, 1917 and with a stamped ticket in hand; Ferddy hopped on the S.P.L.A & S.L.R.R. train and soon arrived in Las Vegas, Nevada.

By this time, the Queen had earned some fame of her own. She was now the madam of her own Las Vegas bar and brothel, called the *Arcade Saloon*. She was now claiming to be Mexican and called herself Juanita Gonzales, or as the locals called her, Mamacita Juanita.

Chapter 6

The Arcade Saloon

The First Railroad Depot in Las Vegas, Nevada 1907

Ten years earlier, in the winter of 1907, the Queen left Storyville and took a two-week Christmas vacation to Los Angeles, California. Her oldest brother, Bill Johnson, owned and operated a cigar store there. Bill was still playing music, and in fact, he was trying to put a new jazz band together.

While visiting her brother, she read an article in a Los Angeles newspaper. The California newspaper hyped the new Las Vegas, Nevada region.

A Los Angeles Daily Times reporter wrote in January 1908, *"The new San Pedro, Los Angeles, and Salt Lake City Railroad unlocks the world to a new territory of fabulous riches. Lots are starting at $100."* The article boasted of an opportunity for minorities and women to become landowners in the new frontier town site called Las Vegas.

Los Angeles Herald c.1908

The Queen was very intrigued by the news article, so she packed a bag and boarded the train. The shiny new rails now stretched along the Old Spanish Trail from Los Angeles to Santa Fe, New Mexico. The train made several stops along the way, including Las Vegas.

She wanted to see for herself what this new town was all about. The Queen was looking for a new adventure and just maybe Las Vegas was the place to find it. The population of this new town was still less than 500 people and the simple thought of it excited her immensely. Even before leaving, The Queen had an idea of what she was looking for. She heard talk about an area called Block 16, a designated area clearly marked on the town map. This was the only location in town where it was legal to sell liquor, and as far as she could tell, no one in that area was in the businesses of prostitution......yet. Block 16 was also near the train depot. She figured she could get some of her customer base from the many passengers who would layover on their journey from Los Angeles to Salt Lake City. This was exactly what she was looking for, and the new Las Vegas region seemed ripe for the picking. Maybe one day Las Vegas could even become the new Storyville.

The Queen was twenty-six years old now and in the prime of her life. Unlike most of the girls back in Storyville, The Queen had saved up a sizeable bankroll. With a plan in mind and a purse full of money, she began surveying the town, hoping to find an established business from which she could operate.

The streets of Las Vegas looked like a set from a Hollywood western movie. It was complete with gun packing, love starved cowboys, lonely old prospectors and swinging door saloons. There were definitely plenty of men trying to quench their nonstop thirst for whiskey and women. With her usual grit and a little luck, The Queen found the perfect place. It was an existing saloon called

The Arcade. The building was at the far end of First Street between Stewart and Odgen. On the front of the building in big letters was the name, **THE ARCADE.**

The Arcade is at the end of the block.

The place wasn't as fancy as the other establishments like The Gem, The Arizona Club, or The Red Onion, but for her purpose, the location was faultless. The Arcade was a long narrow wood-framed building. In the rear of the structure was one big room that she figured could be divided into several smaller rooms. Each small room could

be rented by the hour or by the night, complete with girls if desired. The Queen quickly negotiated a lease with an option to buy the business. She could hardly wait to get back to Storyville to ask a couple of her friends to join her in her new venture.

It wasn't long before The Queen was open for business in Las Vegas. She was now both saloon manager and madam of her own bar/brothel. The girls she hired worked as semi-independent contractors and gave a cut of their profits to The Queen's Arcade. The Arcade had a bar on one side, a dance floor on the other and several small rooms in the back. A dance with a lady would cost $1.00, and when the dance was over, the customer was expected to buy himself a drink, and another one for the lady. His was a strong liquor concoction costing another $1.00 and the lady's special drink (which was nothing more than colored water) added an additional 50¢. The ladies made 25¢ on their drink and 25¢ went to the bar. The Queen's Arcade became one of the first establishments in Las Vegas to openly offer sex for sale, and Block 16 quickly became known as another red-light district.

Bottled liquor was also very lucrative in The Queen's Arcade. On the back bar stood several rows of short-necked flasks. The whiskey flasks were in two sizes. The small one held about 5 ounces, and the larger one held about 10 ounces. These bottles were plainly labeled *two bits* and *four bits*. Cowboys and miners often bought these bottles, because they fit neatly into their pockets or leather chaps. They were often referred to as *glass overcoats*, because the whisky was said to warm the blood on a cold morning. Thousands of these little empty bottles were tossed aside into the Nevada desert. The mule trails, train tracks and roadsides of the Las Vegas landscape, sparkled in the hot sun from the glass of these broken bottles. Block 16 was also a place to get to know people. Not only the locals, but even the civic leaders went there to be seen and heard.

The railroad was one of the historical events that literally helped put the frontier town of Las Vegas on the map. It was built by an enterprising young senator from Montana named William Andrew Clark. Senator Clark was a small wiry man with fiery red hair and a wild red beard. With his boots on, he only stood five feet, four inches tall. Even in the blazing heat of the summer, he was seldom seen without his swallow-tailed coat and top hat. The senator was a banker, a merchant, a land baron and a millionaire by the time he was thirty years old. Clark yearned to be a statesman and had used his newspaper, the *Butte Miner,* to help drive his political ambitions. Clark's lifetime goal had always been to serve in the U.S. Senate, and it later became clear how he managed to

 make that dream become a reality. Evidence would later show Clark had paid over one million dollars in bribes to certain unidentified people to assure his Democratic seat in the U.S. Senate. As a result, it became clear to the senator that money could buy him just about anything he wanted.

It is said that Senator Clark stomped hard on many toes on his way up the ladder to his immense success. Clark was sixty-two when he was elected as Montana's Senator in 1901. Shortly after his election, he met an aspiring actress named Anna Lachapellea. Anna was only fifteen years old when she became pregnant with the Senator's child. He was more than forty-seven years her senior. Because Anna was so young, and for fear of bad publicity, Clark sent young Anna to Paris, France until the child was born. He later married her, and soon after, she had a second child. After Clark won the Senate race, he traveled to the Nevada desert with a specific plan in mind. Clark needed a fast and economical way to transport the ore from his copper mines to the western seaports for exporting.

He wanted to build a railroad that would follow the Old Spanish Trail, a frequently traveled wagon route. This railroad would connect Los Angeles to Salt Lake City and shorten the present travel distance by more than six hundred-thirty miles. A reliable source of water to operate the thirsty steam-driven locomotives was also essential. Las Vegas, (Spanish for 'The Meadows'), seemed an excellent halfway point for the train route since the small community had a large spring and an artesian well. It was a popular water stop for wagon trains and travelers alike.

Senator Clark was able to purchase the *Gass Ranch* from a widow, named Helen Stewart. Mrs. Stewart agreed to sell Senator Clark most of her land and the water rights. Stewart's ranch was 1,834 acres in size and included an artesian well and the Las Vegas Creek, which twisted its way through the ranch. The negotiated price was $55,000 but did not include the family cemetery or a small part of the water from the Las Vegas Creek.

To recoup some of his investment, Clark then divided the newly acquired land and held a public auction to sell lots in the new town site. It was strictly stated in the land deeds that saloons and the sale of liquor were prohibited on any of the town sites, except for block 16 and 17. The railroad offered a special rate of $16.00 for a passenger to come out and look at the new Las Vegas town site. If he or she purchased a lot, the total amount of the ticket was refunded.

The auctioneer, with gavel in hand, called for the auction to begin. Prices ranged from $100.00 to $500.00 for residential and inside lots, and corner lots were as high as $750.00. On the day of the auction, temperatures reached one hundred twelve degrees while more than a thousand people crowded around a wooden platform to shout out what they hoped would be the winning bid. On May 15, 1905, the first day of the auction, one hundred seventy-six lots were sold for a total of $79,566.00. That left the senator with a profit of more than $24,000.00. Over six hundred lots were sold in all, netting the Senator over a quarter of a million dollars.

On July 10, 1909, in honor of Senator Clark, the Nevada Legislature created Clark County. A festive celebration in honor of the senator started with a loud bang from a large cannon. Fireworks burst into the air and the locomotive bells and whistles echoed through the town. It was a daylong picnic-style event complete with wheelbarrow and potato sack races, a baseball game, plenty of food and a band. The temperature rose to well over one hundred degrees and people were in dire need of refreshment. The only businesses that could sell liquor were at the north end of town on Block 16. On that day, all of the saloons including The Queen's Arcade Saloon literally sold out of all of their liquor stock. The celebration continued into the evening with a festive ball at the newly constructed opera house. This event would give the locals a chance to meet and hail the famed senator.

The Queen loved attending parties and was very comfortable in any social situation. With her style and charisma, she was in fact, quite the social butterfly. She attended the ball in honor of Senator Clark where he bragged of his copper mining operation in Jerome, Arizona, and invited everyone to come and visit one day. He also didn't fail to mention he was netting over a million dollars a month just in his Jerome copper enterprise. The Queen always had an eager eye for the dollar, and after hearing that the men in Jerome out-numbered the women ten to one; she now had thoughts of also opening a brothel there someday. For now though, business in the Arcade Saloon was booming and the town was growing fast. By the following year, Las Vegas' population almost doubled. The 1910 U.S. census reported Las Vegas to have nine hundred thirty-seven residents.

Sometime after 1910, The Queen exercised her "option to buy" and took title to the Arcade Saloon. The first thing she did was to add a second story to the building. The Arcade reportedly already had several back rooms for prostitutes, which in fact disturbed some of the local civic leaders. However, after a meeting with The Queen, the leaders preferred to leave the issue alone as long as the businesses on Block 16 kept things orderly and operated in a professional manner. While The Queen's Arcade was one of the first establishments to openly promote prostitution in Las Vegas, it wasn't long before other establishments offered the same services. Almost immediately saloons and brothels were required to pay a $500 license fee and were subject to regular shakedowns and raids.

On March 19, 1911, gambling was legalized on Block 16. A few months later, the Queen acquired her gambling license and the Arcade Saloon then featured the games, Faro and Roulette. Of course, there were still girls to keep a lonely man company, plus music and dancing on the weekends, but now the largest profits were coming from gambling.

Unlike some professions, the gambling business was not strictly a man's domain. Many women, tired of the strict codes and prescribed roles of the Victorian societies, also sought adventure in the gaming houses. Saloonkeepers quickly discovered that a pretty woman dealing the cards boosted business and as a result, many game tables featured a woman behind the dealer's box. Women dealers also tended to keep things safer, because most men wouldn't pull a gun on a woman. Another advantage of a woman dealer was that the men perceived the fairer sex as more honest. Truth be known, it was quite the contrary.

At the time, there were no people of color to speak of in Las Vegas, and The Queen had always struggled with her own racial identity. Being of mixed race, she was always too black to be white and too white to be black. This seemed to be the perfect time to change all that, so she invented a new identity for herself. She claimed to be Mexican and renamed herself Juanita Gonzales. She quickly became well known in the red-light district of Las Vegas as Mamacita Juanita. (*Although not a literal translation, 'Mamacita' is an endearing name in Spanish meaning 'hot sexy little mama.'*)

It's just speculation, but the last name of Gonzales may have been resurrected from the Spanish Madam Antonia P. Gonzalez, for whom The Queen worked back in Storyville.

Mamacita Juanita certainly was hot and sexy. She was also very shrewd. She was undeniably in her element among the scantily clad women with their unfastened morals, the gambling, the hustling and the river of whiskey that flowed through the town. She instinctively knew how to extract money from men and always seemed to be in the right place at the right time. The Arcade was becoming quite a gold mine. Even though the girls were required to be properly dressed on the city streets, most nights you could get a glimpse of a naked woman standing in the upper story window at The Arcade.

The desert town of Las Vegas was worlds apart from the fancy parlor houses in Storyville with which The Queen was so familiar. She remembered the heaping piles of garbage that would accumulate in the back alleys, and the sour stench of the chamber pots that were emptied in the streets. In Storyville, you were lucky to get a tiny breeze and with the impenetrable dampness, nothing ever seemed to dry. In Las Vegas, however, anything that wasn't staked down would simply be blown away by the powerful winds that raged through town. It was also so dry that any liquid spilled on the streets would quickly evaporate.

Making the Change

The New Orleans streets were damp, cold and Musty,

The Las Vegas streets were hot, dry and dusty

The Louisiana top hats and fancy three-piece suits

Gave way to the Nevada's cowboy hats and boots,

Once a bottle of aged fine wine

Now a jar of homemade moonshine,

The mighty Mississippi, was always quite noisy,

This desert town was quiet except for a howling coyotee.

The Storyville 'big shots' with all their boastful chatter,

Replaced by the Cowboy who spoke only when it mattered.

Peggy Hicks

The Queen was making daily deposits at the First State Bank of Las Vegas where she was acquiring quite a substantial bank account. It wasn't long before she was doing so much business that she needed additional help. She sent word to her two brothers, Dink and James Johnson, and before long, reinforcements arrived in Las Vegas. James did odd jobs for a while but was soon drafted into World War I. Dink took on the job of tending bar at the Arcade Saloon in the daytime and played music at night. Dink had a style of music all his own. He gained a reputation as a *barrelhouse piano player. (Barrelhouses were typically underground jazz clubs).*

The Black man in the white coat on the left is believed to be Dink Johnson in the Arizona Club in Las Vegas. c.1914

A long blast from an approaching train echoed across Nevada's desert floor and the locals were open for business. The Los Angeles and Salt Lake train arrived at the Las Vegas depot late in the afternoon on the 10th of February, 1917. As expected, the passengers had about an hour layover as the thirsty locomotives were refilled with water and stocked with coal. The savvy men often headed for block 16 where they could buy a drink, maybe play a fast game of faro or even grab a "quickie" before the train was ready to leave. Some passengers would layover for a day or two before continuing on to Goldfield and then on to Salt Lake City. The Queen watched as the passengers disembarked. Out of the corner of her eye, she noticed a tall, dark, handsomely dressed man with an obvious swagger making his way down the block to her Arcade Saloon. To her surprise it was her old friend from New Orleans she hadn't seen in years, Ferdinand Morton. He had come to visit and check out the new frontier town. He thought he might do a little gambling and maybe even show off his new brand of music.

Unfortunately, the frontier town of Las Vegas was not what Ferddy expected. The cowboys and miners did not take highly to his fast-paced style of music called Jazz. He was even a little intimidated by some of the audiences. In spite of this, Ferddy stayed in Las Vegas for a month or two, making trips back and forth to California to play gigs with some of his old musician friends. Ferddy Morton had been playing in a band called the *Black and Tan Orchestra* at the Cadillac Café on Central Avenue in Los Angeles. One night, Ferddy caught a woman entertainer, named Ada Bricktop Smith, stealing his tips. He confronted her, and a heated battle of words ensued. The boss, overhearing the argument, allegedly scolded Ferddy for "getting his Creole up" (*A common Louisiana phrase for a hot temper*) and settled the argument by firing both of them. Although unfortunate, this incident had no effect on Ferddy, and his career never missed a beat. His music was now in great demand and his most popular song entitled *Jelly Roll Blues* was becoming a big hit.

Soon Ferddy rekindled his relationship with his old girl friend, The Queen. Ferddy now felt that at least he had one thing he so desired, "the pretty girl". The other unsettled business was a band. He wanted to break out and be the leader of his own band and the victor of his own music. He knew he had both the talent and the self-confidence needed to become a big star. Ferddy persuaded the Queen to turn over the management of The Arcade Saloon to her 20 year old little brother, Dink Johnson. Their plan was to travel around and try to get a Jazz band together, and the Queen's Arcade Saloon would supply the grubstake money.

Leaving Dink in charge of the Arcade, Ferddy and the Queen both boarded the San Pedro, Los Angeles and Salt Lake City Railroad back to Los Angeles.

Passengers disembarking the train in Los Angeles, California

Chapter 7

Off to See the World

First and Broadway, Los Angeles, California c. 1917

Once they arrived in Los Angeles, the first thing on the agenda was to purchase a brand new touring car for their newest escapade around the country. With Ferddy in the driver's seat and The Queen by his side, the two of them set off to see the world in flamboyant style.

Jelly Roll showing off his brand new touring car.

The couple decided that along with a new car and a new wardrobe, it also seemed the perfect time for new names. This was in no way out of character for The Queen, since she had changed her name countless times before. She had been using the name Mamacita Juanita Gonzales. This time she dropped Mamacita and the Ju in Juanita, and for the next few years, called herself *Anita Morton* or sometimes *Anita Gonzales*.

Ferddy Morton would now call himself *Jelly Roll Morton*. The nickname *Jelly Roll* was a stage name he acquired while traveling in a vaudeville show. It came from a sexual bragging of sorts and carries various sexual meanings.

Jelly Roll and The Queen always dressed in the most up-to-date fashions complete with expensive tailored clothing and diamond jewelry. Jelly Roll was known to wear bright colored silk shirts, vests, tight pants, short vamp shoes and a Stetson derby. Over the years, Jelly became quite a showman. Before performing, he would meticulously fold up his overcoat, so the expensive plaid lining would show when he placed it on top of the piano. Anita, also impeccably dressed in the latest fashions, would be his assistant. She would often introduce him as the "inventor of jazz" and then sit or lean on the piano while he performed. Traveling the country together, they helped set the trends both in music and in fashion for the new and upcoming jazz age.

In the later part of 1917, the new couple made their first investment together. They purchased a hotel on Central Ave. and 12th St. in Los Angeles and named the place *Anita Hotel*. The hotel turned out to be more like a bordello than a hotel with The Queen again playing the part of the Madam, with a handful of attractive ladies for her employees. Meanwhile, Jelly Roll Morton took over the gambling club next door. By running both the hotel and the nightclub, they single-handedly cornered the market on sin on Central Avenue.

The hotel business however turned out to be disastrous and The Queen blamed Jelly Roll for its failure. She claimed Jelly was too demanding, too protective and intensely jealous. Jelly Roll wouldn't allow Anita to do anything herself, perhaps for fear of getting a little too close to a customer. As a result, they always had to hire help to run the business. At the same time, The Queen thought

Jelly was cheating on her with a performer at the club next door. He didn't trust her, and she didn't trust him, and the pot was about to boil over.

The Queen always had a certain predictable toughness about her and would usually stay the course when there was trouble. Occasionally though, if she didn't like the situation she was in, she would simply turn her back and move on. This was one of those times.

She packed her bags and announced she was selling the Anita Hotel to a woman named Blondie Robinson, for a mere $400.00 and heading for Arizona whether Jelly liked it or not. The Queen remembered her conversation with Senator Clark and thought this would be a good time to explore the opportunities in the booming copper mining town of Jerome, Arizona. She told Jelly that he could tag along if he wanted to, but he couldn't stop her from leaving. Jelly Roll said he had a few irons in the fire right where he was and decided to stay behind in California.

East side of Main Street in Jerome, Arizona c. 1918-1920

Once in Jerome, The Queen easily found work at the Post Office/Cigar Store. She was familiar with tobacco products from working for her brother Bill in his cigar store in Los Angeles. Next, she found a room to rent above the City Café, owned by Nathan Shultz. Nathan also owned the New York Pool Hall and the New York Store, a very well known upscale clothing outlet. It wasn't long before she began to help manage the restaurant along with several small rooms above the café.

The Queen did keep in touch with Jelly Roll, and as usual, was always trying to manipulate him as if he were a child. After all, she was seven years older than Jelly and much more experienced in the dance of courtship. Jelly Roll soon gave in to The Queen, and quickly caught up with her in Jerome, pleading with her to come back.

The Queen, known to the locals as Anita Gonzales, had quickly become involved in Jerome's local community. With her outgoing personality and interest in music, she also became acquainted with some of the local musicians. When Jelly Roll arrived in Jerome, she introduced him to some of her newfound friends.

A local piano player named, George Chilcott, had a small hometown orchestra that provided musical accompaniment for the silent movies and special events in Jerome. One afternoon George invited Jelly Roll to practice with the Chilcott band. Jelly was thrilled. He was always eager to show off his new glitzy jazz style of music to anyone who would listen. George liked what he heard and because of Jelly Roll's influence, George soon spiced up his own music and renamed his orchestra *The Chilly Jazz Band*. The band played mostly at local saloons and dances but also booked engagements at social events in the nearby towns of Prescott and Flagstaff. The Chilly Jazz Band consisted of a standup bass, a trombone, a trumpet, Harry Mader at the drums, and George Chilcott played the piano.

On March 10, 1918, The Queen helped organize a dance to raise money for the World War I Thrift Stamps effort. Tickets were sold for $1.50 and each customer would receive six thrift stamps valued at 25¢ each. Tickets for the dance were sold at the Bank of Arizona, Yavapai Drugs, or could be picked up at the Post Office/Cigar Store where Anita Gonzales worked. *The Jerome War Savings Committee*, as it was called, consisted of a few of Jerome's more prominent community leaders and businessmen. They included Mr. J. E. McLean, Tom Macleod, Clarence Hopkins and A. J. Kisselberg. The event was held at the Jerome Opera House, and the music was provided by George Chilcott and the Chilly Jazz Band. The Verde Copper News printed the tickets free of charge, and local merchants donated prizes for the raffle. The event was a big success.

Allegedly, Jelly Roll Morton sat in with the band and played a couple of his jazz tunes, but ironically, his name was not even mentioned in the next day's newspaper.

Verde Copper News article,
the following Monday March 12, 1918

The Thrift Stamp Dance

Being payday night the streets were jam-packed with people with their pockets jammed with money. So jammed full of features was the thrift stamp dance given by the local committee last Saturday evening that a mere newspaper chronicler scarcely knows where to begin. Was the outstanding feature the validity with which the fairer sex flocked around the roulette tables? Or was it when R. W. Hart won $100 worth of baby bonds? Was it when Alexander Kisselburg raffled off his candy bucket or the diamond ring donated by the Charles C. Robinson Store? There is no question one of the big outstanding features was the delicious white punch served by an impeccably dressed black woman. So many inquiries have been made about that white punch served by 'the black woman' that the Verde copper news took the trouble to ascertain the chemical composition thereof.

Note: The black woman mentioned in the above article may have been Anita Morton, aka. Anita Gonzales. The following is the recipe for the white punch served at the thrift stamp dance. It just so happens, it was The Queen's own recipe and an old New Orleans favorite.

White Punch (White Rum Milk Punch)

An old New Orleans favorite perfect for brunch or to chase away last night's over-indulgence.

Fill glass with crushed ice
Add 1 ½ ounce White Rum
½ ounce simple syrup &
4 ounce fresh whole milk,
Top off with 4 dashes of
real vanilla (not imitation).
Stir and garnish with another
dash of vanilla, and dust with
freshly ground nutmeg.

This recipe may be adjusted for a large crowd or served in a punch bowl. For Virgin White Punch, omit the rum.

This sweet velvety punch was popular in New Orleans in the late 1800s and early 1900s. It was often served on the Mississippi River boats and was a favorite drink at jazz dances and social events.

*A rare picture of Jelly Roll Morton and Anita (Gonzales) Morton
Aka 'The Cuban Queen' c. 1917-1919*

Jelly Roll was extremely jealous of the attention Anita had received at the Thrift Stamp dance. Of course, she rubbed it in, and another argument ensued between the two of them. Jelly Roll didn't care much for the rough mining camps and frontier towns of Las Vegas, Prescott, or Jerome, and in truth they never cared much for him either.

Jelly Roll once said, *"Most of the saloons had small stages at the back of a tall dimly lit narrow room. The acoustics were terrible in those places. The saloons were filled with smoke, rowdy cowboys and dirty miners. And to make it worse, half of them didn't even speak English. You could smell those men with their filthy clothes clear across the room. All those people wanted to do was get drunk and fight and could care less about my music."*

Jelly Roll considered himself an artist and had more important engagements on his mind than the Jerome mining camp. Jerome was a little behind the times and really wasn't quite ready for jazz music. Most of the local miners wanted to hear Mexican folk style music. Although Jerome had many ethnic groups, African American was not one of them. Jelly Roll Morton felt out of place and unwelcomed, and his jazz music was certainly unappreciated. He wanted to make a name for himself in the world of jazz, and Jelly knew Jerome was not the place to do it. He preferred the bright lights and more civilized attractions found in the big cities. After the argument with The Queen, Jelly packed up his things and headed back to California, and The Queen remained in Jerome.

For The Queen, it was a different story. She was accustomed to the miner and cowboy lifestyle. After all, she spent almost eight years as Mamacita Juanita, the madam of the Arcade Saloon in Las Vegas. She had no problem fitting into Jerome's rowdy crowd. There was plenty of opportunity for her kind of work right where she was.

By now, Jerome was bursting with action and copper was in high demand because of World War I. The mines were running three shifts a day, some restaurants were open twenty-four hours and rooms were being rented by the shift. Money was changing hands everywhere and some people were even getting rich.

The Queen, trying to get in on some of the action, bought several shares of Monster Chief Mining Company stock. Unfortunately, things didn't work out so well. The business enterprise she heavily bought into, turned out to be a fraudulent wildcat company scam, and she lost her entire investment. Shortly after that, she lost her job managing the City Café when a fire destroyed the kitchen and several of the upstairs rooms. If things couldn't get any worse, there was now a new lawman in town. Sheriff John Crowley was appointed and part of his job was to clean up the prostitution. It's reported that in one day he personally rounded up more than forty sporting ladies from the red-light district and ran them out of town. His conquest was short lived though. A few days later, most of the girls drifted back into town. It was indeed getting more and more difficult to be in the business of prostitution in Jerome. Sheriff Crowley would later show to be quite a force to be reckoned with.

As usual, The Queen and Jelly Roll Morton couldn't be apart for very long. After several highs and lows for the both of them, they found themselves together once again. Her new plan was to rejoin Jelly Roll in California and this time Jelly and The Queen were talking marriage. She wanted to surprise Jelly Roll with a special gift to celebrate Christmas and their reconciliation. Before leaving Jerome and heading back to Jelly's world in California, she liquidated all her investments and withdrew her money from the bank. She then made one last purchase at her favorite store. She splurged and bought a beautiful 30-point diamond from Jerome's upscale jewelry store on Main Street called *Chas Robinson Jewelers*. The diamond cost her a little over a thousand dollars, a tidy sum in 1918. She then gave that diamond to Jelly Roll Morton as a Christmas/wedding present.

Jelly Roll immediately had the diamond set in gold and implanted in his front tooth. He then made a promise to Anita. He said, *"I'll never remove this diamond as long as I live, and it will always be a symbol of my love for you."*

This diamond-studded tooth soon became one of Jelly's major trademarks. When Jelly Roll would perform, the diamond would sparkle in the stage lights.

Before long, the impulsive couple bought into another business in San Francisco called the *Jupiter Night Club*. The nightclub was located on Columbus Avenue between Pacific and Jackson. The Queen spent a great deal of her time and money redecorating the club. The establishment gained a reputation for lively entertainment by the *Black and Tan Band,* led by Jelly Roll Morton himself. The Queen handled the bar and the waitresses, and Jelly Roll provided the music. One night, with his aggressive personality, Jelly Roll got into a heated argument with the local police and the authorities ended up banishing him from his own nightclub. Now, with The Queen at the helm, Jelly then spent a considerable amount of time and money traveling between San Francisco and Los Angeles. Jelly Roll never had much respect for money and would usually spend it or lose it as fast as he made it. He loved "the ponies" and usually lost considerable amounts of money at the track. It wasn't long before jealousy reared its ugly head again, and between that and Jelly Roll's gambling, the Jupiter Night Club went bankrupt.

The Queen, who always watched the financial end of things, was unable to control the money and was fed up with everything. One day, while Jelly Roll was away at the racetrack, she took what money remained and slipped out of town. She left word for Jelly Roll that she was heading up north to the gold rush in Alaska where the men outnumbered the women twenty-five to one. She hinted that she was going to do a little mining there of her own.

In other words was, she was going to seek her fortune by shoveling out the pockets of some cold lonely Alaskan miners. Once Jelly Roll got the news, he jumped on a train and headed for the Pacific Northwest after her. That always seemed to be this couple's *modus operandi*. She would leave, and he would go chasing after her. It's interesting to note, that even though Jelly Roll often referred to Anita as his wife and referred to Dink and Bill Johnson as his brothers-in-law, no legal document has ever surfaced to validate a legal marriage between them.

Jelly Roll finally caught up with her in a rooming house in Tacoma, Washington. All she had to say was *"Baby, I just wanted you to pay me some attention. I never really wanted to go to Alaska."* They talked all night, and by morning they decided to try it again. They agreed that maybe a little time in Alaska might be just the thing they needed. After a week or so touring in Alaska, they headed back south to Vancouver.

It was the spring of 1920 in Canada, and Jelly Roll was playing at a nightclub called the *Patty Sullivan Club*. One night, the band's female vocalist became ill and couldn't perform. Anita was a very good singer of ragtime and blues, so she took the microphone and filled in for the sick girl. This made Jelly so angry, he stopped playing the piano right in the middle of the song. Anita kept on singing with the band and finished the number. The audience went wild with applause, and the tip jar on the stage was overflowing with money.

Jelly Roll was never one to be upstaged. He was extremely conceited and needed to be the only one in the spotlight. He was so infuriated at her, that he pulled her outside the club and sternly instructed her never to sing or dance again in his presence. He told her not to even tap her toe to the music. He wanted her to simply sit there, look pretty, endorse him and make him look good. Jelly Roll was obsessed with making his name well known in the music world, whatever it took. Their adventures together would take them from the east coast to the west coast, then north to Canada and Alaska and south to Tijuana, Mexico. Jelly Roll performed in all types of venues and made music wherever they went.

Jelly Roll had a very contentious personality and was also very controlling. This always made it extremely hard to do business with him. The only thing it seemed he could not control, however, was The Queen. He was infatuated with her mysterious charm, her buxom beauty and her sensuality. He admired her calculating business sense and the way she embraced vice as a way of life. Her seductive charm and intelligence kept Jelly Roll coming back time after time. The Queen on the other hand, with her self-sufficient traditions, depended on no man for love or money. The couple had another clash about two months later. Rumor has it she was drunk and accused Jelly Roll of cheating on her again. She picked up a large steak plate and broke it over his head. This time it was the last straw, and both decided to go their separate ways, permanently.

Jelly went east and The Queen went west. Jelly Roll went to New York for a while. He later returned to Chicago, and it was there that Jelly Roll really hit his stride. He was now making a lot of money and knew how to show it off. He literally adorned himself with diamonds and gold from head to toe. Diamonds glimmered on all his fingers, on his tie pin, on his watch, on his belt buckle and even on his sock supports. His diamond studded gold tooth became a

legend of its own. While most musicians were wearing black tuxedos, Jelly wore an expensive wine-colored jacket with white trousers and black and white shoes. Jelly Roll Morton became a trendsetter and was now at the top of the heap.

Jelly Roll Morton made his first recording of piano solos for the Gennett label. He later formed a band called *The Red Hot Peppers*. The band played New Orleans style jazz. It is said they were the first band to arrange music to fit the exact playing time of a 78-rpm record. Morton reached the height of his popularity between 1926 and 1930. Although music was his first line of business, he was also a renowned gambler, a pool hustler, a vaudeville comedian and a pimp.

The Queen headed back to Las Vegas, Nevada, where her brother, Dink, was still running the Arcade Saloon. It had always been a gold mine for her, but it was now time to turn the page on Las Vegas. She sold the Arcade and with a purse full of money, she headed back to Jerome.

Her plan was to open a new boarding house/brothel like they had never seen before. After all, this was the business she knew so well. She was an expert at making a comfortable living off of other people's weaknesses, like liquor, gambling and sex. The Queen was now a woman who insisted on living like royalty with all of its comforts and freedoms. Unafraid of sin and repercussion, she was determined to get her share of the wild and wicked, "Billion Dollar Copper Camp" called Jerome.

Chapter 8

The Wickedest Town

*The New York Sun newspaper proclaimed Jerome, Arizona
to be "The Wickedest Town in the West"*

Jerome's many saloons were crowded day and night with all kinds of men...but only one kind of woman. Most men carried a deck of cards in their pocket and a revolver tucked in their boot. In fact, gambling in Jerome was said to have become an epidemic.

This wild mining town was located in Central Arizona on the east slope of Mingus Mountain in Yavapai County.

The camp clung treacherously to the steep slope of the hillside and was built atop a vast copper deposit. The mining operation took place in a maze of tunnels that zigzagged back and forth deep below ground. The nearby copper smelter constantly belched a thick toxic haze that fogged the town and choked its inhabitants. The noxious pollution killed vegetation for miles around. This, however, did not stop the thousands of entrepreneurs from making their way to Jerome for their share of the riches. The wealth derived from Jerome's vast mineral deposits attracted people from all walks of life. The streets were filled with miners, bootleggers, gamblers, lawmen, businessmen, preachers, politicians and prostitutes.

The first to occupy this region long ago were the prehistoric Native Americans known as the Anasazis, the Sinaguas and the Hohokams. These native people had a series of crudely worked mines that peppered the hillsides. They too were after the rich blue-green copper minerals including Turquoise, Azurite, Malachite and Chrysocolla. The Spanish followed seeking gold, but instead found copper.

In 1876, three Anglo prospectors staked the first claims on the copper deposits. In 1883, the United Verde Copper Company bought the claims. Then, five years later in 1888 William A. Clark, a wealthy man from Butte, Montana, leased the rights and bought control of most of the mining. Within two decades, Clark was netting over a million dollars a month from his Jerome enterprise.

The town, which began as little more than a mining camp, was hastily built with flimsy wooden structures and numerous canvas tents. The town caught fire and was almost burned out three times between 1897 and 1899. Each time Jerome burned though, it was quickly rebuilt. The dry lumber used for building always provided plenty of fuel for the next devastating inferno. In 1899, the city planners quickly incorporated, so they could add a fire department. A building code was also adopted specifying that brick or masonry must be used in construction. The fires, however, continued. Even the luxurious brick and stone built Montana Hotel, owned by Senator William Clark, was totally gutted by fire in 1915. The fire was so intense, the entire structure was lost.

A fire on June 6, 1917, burned an entire block, including boarding houses and homes, displacing over ninety families. Then, in 1918, another fire burned sixty homes in *the gulch*. That same year there was a huge fire that started in *Mexican Town* and worked its way up to Hull Avenue consuming everything in its path. Losses included a barn and a stable owned by McMillan's Funeral Services. McMillan kept his horse-drawn funeral carriages in the barn and two pair of prize horses in the stable.

The burned out barn sat vacant for a few years until 1922 when *The Cuban Queen Boarding House/Bordello* would rise from its ashes. Yavapai County records show that McMillan owned these lots in block 14 since 1904.

A Prescott Newspaper reported: "Fire, Fire, Fire, Jerome burns again! Entire business district burns completely destroying 24 saloons, 14 chink restaurants, several gambling halls and a handful of bordellos were burned to the ground." c. 1899

Shady Ladies working in tents

Brothels were plentiful in Jerome. If money was an issue, there were also countless shady ladies working in tents, out of wagons and even behind bushes with blankets on the ground. This rough and tumble town was not for the faint of heart. Men outnumbered women ten to one, but there were still ample numbers of "liberal ladies" to tend to the miners who were willing to pay for their services.

There were over a hundred working prostitutes in the scattered bordellos and plenty more in the *cribs* area. The cribs in Jerome were tiny, dark, dismal places consisting of one small room with a bed and a nightstand.

On the nightstand was a small pan or a bowl for washing. This pan contained a type of sanitizer and was called a *Peter Pan*. The ladies would first wash the man's genitals, then squeeze and milk them to check for signs of venereal disease or infection before performing their service. Through experience, the majority of these women could spot a problem even before a doctor could.

A customer was not expected to remove anything but his hat, and often a man would keep his boots on and just pull his trousers down to his knees. The women usually kept a piece of oilcloth or a rug draped over the foot of the bed to keep muddy boots from soiling the bedding.

Whatever the cribs in *Husband's Alley* lacked in quality, they certainly made up in volume. Payday in Jerome was always a busy day for the ladies in the cribs. Competition was fierce and that's what tended to keep the prices low. But even at a mere two bits per encounter, most women were making more money than the laborers in the copper mines. It wasn't unusual for a crib prostitute to service twenty-five or thirty customers on a payday.

Often the men who visited the cribs were even lower class than the women providing the service. These men were sometimes the town's social outcasts. Regulars who visited included drunkards, drug addicts, the sickly or even severely physically or mentally handicapped. Others were simply just filthy, foul smelling men. All were welcomed in the cribs as long as they had money. Some of the women put their names on the cribs, so visitors would know where to find them. Generally, a woman in the cribs worked for herself without a pimp or a madam.

Times were changing, and Jerome soon had its own doctors, lawyers, morticians, jewelers and every other business a city of this size would have. Jerome also had its own city hall, complete with a city council. They wrote their own ordinances and zoning restrictions and hired officials to enforce them. This was no longer just another mining camp.

TOWN OF JEROME
LICENSE TAX RECEIPT
HOUSES OF PROSTITUTION

THIS IS TO CERTIFY That_____

`    ` ____this day paid the sum of_____DOLLARS

being the monthly license tax imposed by ordinance upon 'HOUSES OF PROSTITUTION, and the said

_____is hereby authorized to carry on a House

of Prostitution at_____, from the first day of_____

19 ____, until the first day of_____, 19 ____.

`        ` Dated this_____ day of_____ ____, 19 ____.

_____ `                    ` _____
`        ` Town Clerk `                                        ` Town Mayor

New zoning ordinances were now in effect for the red-light section of town. A brothel inspector was appointed and was paid $7.50 per month to make sure the new laws were enforced. The town of Jerome required the houses of prostitution to be located at least two blocks from Main Street. The ladies must not promote their business by *barking* or calling out, and they must be properly dressed while on the city streets. A house of prostitution was also required to purchase a tax license. All the so-called working women had to register with the town and have a physical examination every two weeks.

There had been many madams in Jerome before the Queen arrived in the early 1920's. There was *Madam Lil* of the Black Cat, *Madam Pearl*, (who was never without a cigarette), and a tall dark-skinned woman they called *Madam Rose*. One of the most famous madams was *Jennie Bauters*. She owned a considerable amount of property in Jerome including a place in the middle of town called *Belgian Jennie's, The Honky-Tonk House of Light Love.*

By the 1890s, it was said that Jennie was the richest madam in the Arizona Territory. Unfortunately, things went awry in 1905 when she took up with an opium addict named Clement C. Leigh. Clement brutally murdered Jennie in Gold Road, Arizona, a small town near Kingman.

As the alleged story goes, Jennie was working in a saloon when Clement approached her and asked for money. She refused. The next morning, Clement, all hopped up on opium, demanded that Jennie loan him some money and again she refused. Clement became agitated, pulled out a gun and began shooting at her. Jennie was still dressed in her nightgown as she ran down the dusty road begging pitifully for her life, *"For God's sake, C. C., please, please don't shoot me!"* Clement responded by empting his gun on Jennie, shooting her in the hip and face and mortally wounding her. The pain on her once pretty, but now twisted and contorted face said it all as she made the sign of the cross and died on the dirt road that morning.

Eyewitnesses said that even after Jennie was dead, Clement C. Leigh went into the nearby saloon and demanded a shot of whiskey. He quickly reloaded his gun and returned to the scene. He walked up to Jennie's lifeless body, shoved her head to the side with his foot and shot her again. Clement then turned the gun on himself and fired a bullet into his own chest. He lay down beside Jennie and covered his face with his hat expecting to die. Ironically, Clement C. Leigh easily survived his self-inflicted wound only to face trial and was later hung for his murderous crime.

Most folks characterized Jennie as a generous and kind person, particularly toward the down-and-out miners and prospectors. Jennie Bauters's estate was worth a tidy sum. It included five lots and a building in Jerome, plus rents and sizeable bank accounts.

Arizona Republican Newspaper
November 2, 1905

The crime was a brutal one, but the friends of the murderer believe there was some measure of justification, or rather that there were some mitigating circumstances by reason of which they think the sentence was too severe and that the ends of justice might be satisfied with a lesser penalty than expiation in the gallows. It is said the woman was employed in a saloon probably as a singer or to encourage the selling of drinks. Leigh had approached her and asked for money, which she declined to advance to him, and they quarreled for some time when he became desperate and began shooting.

The victim was Jennie Bauters who had lived in Jerome for several years and was a person of notorious character. Leigh had lived with her for some time in Jerome and later at Acme Camp near Gold Road in Mohave County where the killing took place. It was alleged that on the morning of the shooting, September 3 of this year, they had quarreled over money matters and that Leigh had shot the woman down and that while she lay, probably mortally wounded on the ground, he reloaded his weapon and standing over her, fired again killing her instantly. He then turned the weapon on himself and sent a bullet into his left breast but the wound did not prove a serious one.

Clement C. Leigh's story differs somewhat in respect of the most brutal details though there is a frank admission of the murder. He says he was passing a tent in which the woman lived (there being nothing but tent houses in the camp) when she called to him to give her a cigarette. He did so and entering the tent, they began quarreling about another man with whom the woman desired to live in preference to him. The end of it was that she called him a vile name and started to run away saying she was going after a gun to kill him. He became uncontrollably angered and shot her. He does not know for sure how many times he shot her but he says he was at least fifteen feet away when the last shot was fired.

He then shot himself partly because he thought he had got into serious trouble by killing her and partly because he did not care to live after she was dead.

The local newspaper reported: January 21 1907

"The trap-door sprung at precisely 2:00 in the afternoon of January 18, 1907 and Clement Leigh plunged to his death for the murder of Jennie Baunters. After hanging for thirty minutes, he was pronounced dead and cut down. Clement C. Leigh was buried at the county's expense in Kingman, Arizona.

Cleopatra Hill, as it was named, looked almost like a house of cards ready to tumble down at any moment. The wealthiest citizens, like the mining engineers and executives, were living in company houses at the top of the hill. The further down the mountain you lived, the lower the class of citizen you probably were. That's just the way it was. Sanitation was lacking and in most areas, indoor plumbing was rare. There were mounds of garbage accumulating everywhere. In some areas, men were simply urinating off the porches. The women, being a little more discrete, would go into a closet and use a chamber pot. But then, often after a full day of use, they would pour the foul mixture out a window or over a balcony only to land on the house or the property just below. Because of these unsanitary practices, diseases became abundant. Epidemics like Smallpox, Scarlet Fever and the Spanish Influenza ran rampant. Something had to be done.

Enter Ordinance No.85.

[*Ordinance No. 85 was approved on December 11th, 1917, by Mayor J. J. Cain and Common Council. This ordinance allowed the health officer to restrict any putrid or unwholesome water or offensive substance that causes an odor or stench, to raise there from. Anyone who violated this ordinance was given a thirty-day notice to cease and desist. If this person violated the provisions of this ordinance and was convicted, they were subject to a fine of not less than $10.00 or more than $100.*]

People wore gauze masks to help stop the spread of the Spanish Influenza. Recent genetic studies have concluded that the Spanish Flu was closely related to the Swine Flu and is believed to been transmitted back and forth between swine and humans.

In October of 1918, more than two hundred fifty people in Jerome had contracted the Spanish Flu and seventy-five people reportedly died from the disease. A strict quarantine was issued and for several weeks, armed guards were stationed on all roads leading to and from Jerome. The United Verde Hospital in Jerome was full to capacity and temporary beds had to be placed in the public schools. Everyone was forced to wear gauze masks and all town functions were canceled. During its ten-month duration, an estimated thirty million people perished worldwide from the Spanish Influenza epidemic. Estimates place the death toll in the United States at over six hundred seventy-five thousand with over twenty-two million becoming ill. That was more than twice the number killed during the First World War.

Being the dangerous place that it was, death in Jerome also came in other forms. It could be a quick strike from a rattlesnake, being in the wrong place during a gunfight, or killed in a mining accident. One could even have been crushed to death by a runaway mule team as they pulled heavy wagons of copper ore down Main Street.

The town was mostly made up of hastily built saloons, restaurants, wooden shacks and tents. The devastating fires of the past had left a shortage of places to eat and sleep. Jerome had over eight thousand men working in the underground tunnels, and the majority of the laborers were of Mexican descent. Old-timers say that when the shift whistle blew, hundreds of men came up from "that man-made hell." The miners looked like a huge army of ants with blackened faces. They were cold, tired and hungry, all looking for a place to eat and rest after a hard day's work.

The lucky few had wives and hot meals waiting for them, but most workers went to boarding houses or restaurants. Some drank their supper at one of the local saloons and others mostly did without.

The unskilled immigrants were often the ones assigned to the most dangerous tasks. Men were often crippled when they fell down shafts, were jerked from hoist cages, or were crushed while working under unstable rock that collapsed without warning. Some of these men lost limbs or had become disfigured from exploding dynamite charges. Many were maimed by the debris from the blasts and others were injured from the manmade earthquakes that collapsed tunnels or brought entire buildings down. There was reportedly an ordinance specifically adopted for the many injured or maimed men of Jerome. The ordinance required that these misfortunate citizens must always use the alleyways to travel about town. They were ordered to avoid the main streets as not to cause fright to the women and children. Most respectable women seldom walked the streets alone for fear of being kidnapped or worse, and they always kept their children close at hand.

By the late 1920s, Jerome became the fourth largest city in Arizona, boasting a population of over fifteen thousand. This former "camp town" had become a twenty-four-hour city with mine operations running three shifts per day. Jerome had numerous hotels, boarding houses, several grocery stores, hardware stores and a saloon on every corner. There were also two theaters, a bowling alley and an abundance of billiard and gambling halls.

The Phoenix Enterprise newspaper wrote, "Jerome saloons are crowded day and night by gamesters, and gambling has become epidemic." The paper went on to say, "Jerome is <u>not</u> a city of churches."

By the time The Queen returned to Jerome in 1921, it was the beginning of a new decade and things were looking up. The copper camp had tripled in size and had become a bustling city. The war was over, the Spanish Flu was disappearing as quickly as it came, and the people of Jerome were looking forward to a new decade of health, wealth and prosperity.

Once again, The Queen seemed to be in the right place at the right time. With her good looks and her keen business savvy, her plan was to take Jerome by storm, and she set out to do just that.

Chapter 9

And All That Jazz

The Cuban Queen ruled in Jerome for a decade, during the Roaring Twenties.

The Roaring Twenties was a decade filled with flappers, bootleggers, riotous living, gambling, and jazz music. It was in the late summer of 1921 when the Queen made her way back to Jerome. She arrived in Clarkdale, Arizona, on the new standard gauge railroad built by Senator Clark. Clarkdale, a town that bore Senator Clark's name was designed and built from a unified master plan. The town was designed to have every possible modern convenience. There was telephone, telegraph, water, sewer and up-to-date electrical services. The streets were wide and there were buildings for all types of businesses and professionals. She heard there were even subsidized homes for some of the mining community. This was quite unlike the place she was headed with its haphazard array of structures hanging to the side of a mountain.

She must have turned a few heads when she stepped off the train in Clarkdale. She looked as if she had just walked off the front page of a roaring '20s fashion magazine. There in the depot, she lit her new Marlboro cigarette with its bright red 'beauty tip.' *(The cigarette was marketed to women in the '20s and had a red ribbon around the end so as not to show lipstick smears.)* She was wearing the latest jazz age fashions from the trend-setting state of California. Under her arm, she carried a beaded handbag decorated in a beautiful motif that matched her outfit. Her well-guarded handbag contained an expensive French perfume, blood red lipstick and a considerable amount of cash.

The over-stated fragrance of her rose-scented perfume was suddenly and rudely replaced by a belch of thick black smoke as the train slowly pulled out of the station. The wide-eyed porter checked her one-way ticket, retrieved her overstuffed bags and travel trunk and carefully stacked them on the freight wagon. They would be transported up the mountain from Clarkdale to Jerome. She smiled, reached into her beaded handbag and handed him a shiny new quarter. Scarcely able to take his eyes off her, he tipped his hat and mumbled shyly, *"Thank you madam. You have a pleasant day now, ya hear?"*

Fast forward: An excursion train, called the Verde Canyon Railroad, now operates a scenic four-hour rail journey on the fore mentioned original railroad tracks. The train ride starts at the old mining town of Clarkdale, Arizona and then travels along the banks of the Verde River to the Perkinsville Ranch and back again.

The town's people of Jerome had never seen the likes of a tall dark beauty like this before. Her skirt was a little short, and her curly coal black hair was straightened and cut into a short *bob*. A pair of spit curls swept forward at her jaw-line. The Queen, now creating yet another alias, took back her maiden name of Johnson and started calling herself Annie Johnson. Annie, now in her thirties, had acquired quite a fashionable wardrobe during her travels with Jelly Roll Morton.

The Queen spoke in warm tones and carried herself with an unshaken confidence. She was always dressed to the hilt when she went gallivanting around town and used an extreme amount of makeup including her red ox-blood lipstick that she often applied in public. She was rarely seen without her expensive furs and diamond jewelry. She used a type of bleaching cream to lighten her skin and another product to straighten her hair, apparently an attempt to deny her African heritage. She flattened her bust and hips to give her that long slim look known as *Garconne* (meaning boyish in French). Her sleeveless chiffon dresses had a dropped waistline and the dark stockings that covered her shapely legs were made of the new artificial silk they were calling *Rayon*. Her black shoes had ankle straps and Cuban heels. She kept her snugly fit hat, called a *cloche,* pulled stylishly low on her forehead. All this was the new look and was nothing like the stodgy old Victorian fashions that the women of Clarkdale and Jerome were still wearing.

Many have heard the horror stories of the distructive effects corsets had on the female body. When lacing up the corset, one could exert up to eighty pounds of crushing force on a woman's waist, sometimes literally displacing internal organs. The feminine movement had a strong effect on women's fashion and as a result, styles became less formal. The corest was discarded for the first time in centuries and a more masculine look became popular.

The locals often thought of her as a little fast and somewhat brazen. That was probably because she had a way of teasing men with her flirtatious behavior to get what she wanted. That technique worked quite well for The Queen. She had been perfecting those types of manipulation skills long before she found her way back to Jerome. Whatever morals she previously possessed had been progressively lost while working as a sporting lady in Storyville, New Orleans, and as the madam of the Arcade Saloon in Las Vegas.

As a younger woman, she participated in many exotic dances along with burlesque and vaudeville shows. There was also her many experiences with the underground world while traveling with Jelly Roll Morton. These things, among others, molded the Queen into what she had now become.

The Queen loved to dance, and sometimes provocatively. She knew all of the latest dances like the Tango, the Shimmy, the Charleston and the Foxtrot. Her evening dresses were often embellished with sequins and fringe that emphasized her exotic movements while dancing. She especially liked the new dance called the Black Bottom Stomp. Jelly Roll Morton had written the tune called The Black Bottom Stomp and soon after its release, a dance with its namesake emerged.

The dance became a sensation and ended up overtaking the popularity of the Charleston and eventually became the number one social dance of its time. It was with the Red Hot Peppers on the Victor label that Jelly Roll recorded the hit. The dance was fast-paced, energetic and when she danced to it, her sequined dress would shimmer in the lights on the dance floor. She frequented Jerome's many local nightclubs and speakeasies.

The woman in the white dress is Bessie Julia Johnson. It is believed she went by the name 'Annie Johnson' aka 'Cuban Queen' for the decade she resided in Jerome. This photo was taken in the mid '20s, possibly in Jerome.

The term 'speakeasy' became popular during the 1920s to identify bars, restaurants, halls and ballrooms where alcoholic drinks were sold illegally. Speakeasies were typically presented as an ice cream parlor, pastry shop, restaurant or coffee shop. To be admitted in an establishment that served alcoholic beverages, customers had to have the right card, knock or password. They were expected to speak low or discretely in order not to attract attention. Hence the term speakeasy was born.

Needless to say, the Queen fit right in with this wild and wicked boomtown. But the main reason for being in Jerome was business, and if it required a little flirtation and rubbing elbows with the right people, she was up for the task. Like a spider in a web, The Queen was always on the lookout for new prey, but right now she was looking for just the right property in which to operate. It is believed that she acquired a couple of lots in the red-light district just two blocks off Main Street. One of the many devastating fires had burned the existing structures to the ground. An architect drew up plans to make sure her future two-story building would fit perfectly on the steep incline of her newfound Jerome property. All of the necessary permits were obtained and the construction of the new building started almost immediately.

The views of the valley below were spectacular. A set of wide wooden stairs led from the balcony to the lower level where the crib rooms were located. The building was intended to maximize use of every available square foot. On the lower level there were several cramped cribs designed precisely for their function and each with its own private entrance. The upper level contained the main living quarters, kitchen, parlor and a card room. The building had two front doors on the upper street level. While most of the buildings in this area were hastily built entirely of wood, this new building was constructed of concrete, brick and stucco. The stucco was painted a rich apricot color and trimmed with polished sheet copper. At the back of the building was a balcony that also doubled as a working man's sleeping quarters. The Cuban Queen's boarding house was completed in 1922. A few years later, electric was added and one end of the balcony became an outside communal bathroom containing a sink, commode and a claw-foot bathtub. Some said it was one of the most beautifully styled buildings in town.

The Queen, now claiming to be Cuban, would call the new business *The Cuban Queen Boarding House*. As time went on, most of the locals became quite aware that the boarding house was a little more than what the name implied. The Queen always employed girls for their beauty, hoping to attract the more affluent clientele. The interior was fitted with the finest furnishings and fixtures that Jerome had to offer. The inside parlor was decorated with fine carpets, elegant velvet flocked wallpaper and ample mirrors. It was also the only bordello in Jerome that featured gambling. The card tables were always busy with gentlemen engaging in a good game of poker or Faro. The Cuban Queen's place was a cut above the rest and became a very popular place.

The Queen was definitely one to keep up with the times, and any modern flapper would not be complete without an innovative Victrola on which to play her latest 78-rpm jazz records. The Queen became a frequent shopper for music and jewelry at the *Charles C. Robinson Store.* She had purchased Jelly Roll's diamond there just a few years earlier. Charles (*Chas*) knew her well and welcomed her back.

Charles C. Robinson was a fine Jeweler and a man of means. Friends and family called him Chas. Barely standing 5'-5" tall and a little on the portly side, he owned and operated his store at 317 Main Street. His Victrolas ranged

in price from small tabletop models selling for $15.00 to a more stylish model for $100.00. He could also order a Chippendale model that cost as much as $600. This model was designed for the most elegant of mansions. It had a Queen Anne style cabinet and was made from the finest hardwoods with authentic gold trim.

Chas sold expensive jewelry, the latest records and also showcased an extensive line of phonographs and a brand new contraption called a *Radiola*. He proudly advertised that both his phonographs, and his new Radiolas, could be bought on store credit. Chas was happy to sell the Queen both an Orthophonic Victrola and the brand new Radiola.

In 1928, Charles C. Robinson applied for and received a license to build a radio station in the copper town of Jerome, Arizona. The station's call letters were KCRJ. 'K' designates stations west of the Mississippi River. 'CR' stood for Charles Robinson. 'J' stood for either Jeweler or Jerome. No one really knows. KCRJ was licensed to broadcast on a frequency of 1310 kilocycles on the Central Arizona Broadcasting System. The KCRJ radio station became *The Voice of the Verde Valley* and continued to broadcast until 1944.

(During the 1920s, radio stations were being created at incredible speeds reaching more and more people, and helping to spread not only news but the popularity of jazz, rag-time and blues music. People tuned in everyday to listen to music, sports, news and live events. Many artists were heard nationally and even discovered by airing their music on radio stations. The radio also provided a medium for jazz devotees to hear bands from many cities.)

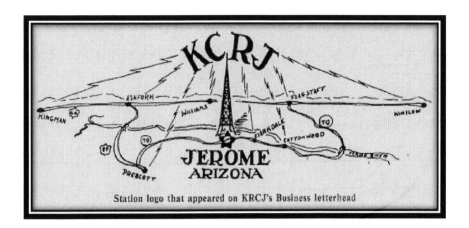
Station logo that appeared on KRCJ's Business letterhead

The Queen's brand new Victrola stood proudly in the corner of the bordello parlor accompanied by a large collection of 78-rpm records. Of course, she played her collection of 78-rpm recordings of the Red Hot Peppers band that Jelly Roll sent to her. The records brought back many memories of her old acquaintances. Her new Radiola connected her to the world outside of Jerome. The Queen loved to listen to the Radiola and would often sing along with the music as if she had recorded the song herself.

One of The Queen's favorite sayings was, *"With jazz I was born to dance and with blues I was born to mourn."* Her favorite songs were from a very popular 1920s female African/American blues and ragtime singer named *Bessie Smith*, also known as, *The Empress of the Blues*. This was quite fitting since The Queen's real name was also Bessie. She could now hear her namesake and all of her favorite singers on her new radio.

The Queen ran her new business like a well-greased wheel. She was an excellent hostess and cook and her customers could expect good meals, the latest music and a good time. She was also quite aware of the occasional need to grease some of the other wheels in town, namely the political wheels.

Old timers of Jerome remembered Annie Johnson *(The Cuban Queen)* as a beautiful tall dark-skinned, buxom woman, possibly mulatto with a southern accent. She was the only madam to have gambling in her bordello. Some said she was a little mysterious and rumor had it she was deeply rooted in the practice of the voodoo traditions.

An anonymous source said, "Her place was known as The Cuban Queen Boarding House, but most everyone knew what it really was. One thing was for sure. If the pretty girls didn't keep you coming back, her fine southern cooking would. A lot went on behind the closed doors of The Cuban Queen. Prostitution, gambling, bootlegged whiskey and God knows what else went on in there. It was a rather popular place, but, very high-priced."

Postcard : Main Street, Jerome, Arizona   c. 1919

Photo: 317 Main Street, Jerome, Arizona   c. 2011

The building is still standing where Charles C. Robinson's jewelry and radio station operated. The building is now owned by the Jerome Historical Society and is occupied by a gift/rock shop called "Arizona Discoveries."

Chapter 10
The Sheriff and the Pie

The Queen added a secret ingredient in her pie that made it taste like no other.

The Cuban Queen was an excellent cook and judging by the southern quality of her recipes, she probably acquired some of her cooking skills from her mother and grandmother. Both these women had worked as cooks in the master's kitchens on large southern plantations. The Queen, being very particular about how she wanted things done at her bordello, did a lot of the work herself. This was especially true when it came to making her baking powder biscuits and the homemade pies that were served on a regular basis.

The Cuban Queen's Kitchen

The Cuban Queen rolled out her piecrust on a small wooden table covered with flour. Using her forearm, she wiped the sweat from her brow as she glanced out the kitchen window at the incredible view. There was a small, peaceful farming community roughly twenty-five miles to the north where the air looked crisp and clean. It was unlike Jerome where the noxious smoke was so prevalent. Her mind wandered a bit as she thought about how nice it would be to live in a place like that. She quickly reminded herself, though, that Jerome was where the money was and that's why she was here. The Queen was in fact looking forward to a very special delivery wagon from that same farming community sometime today.

A Sedona Peach Orchard   c. 1920s

(Many orchards and farms sprang up in the virgin bottom, red soil of the small farming community now called Sedona. The area soon became the breadbasket that helped feed the hungry Jerome population. The fruit orchards flourished and expanded beyond local needs. The surplus produce was shipped by train throughout the southwest. Carl Schnebly was one of the successful farmers who marketed his produce in Jerome. The farming community was later named Sedona after the farmer's wife, Sedona Arabella Miller Schnebly.)

Continuing her task at hand, she carefully folded the large circle of flat pie dough in half and placed it into a pie tin. She frowned when she saw the pitted sides and rusted bottom of her tin, but it would have to do for now. She wiped the flour from her hands on her thin cotton apron. Then, licking her two middle fingers, she touched the hot cast-iron cook stove to gauge its temperature.

The spit on her fingers sizzled from the heat. Even though the summer's mid-morning temperature was well on its way to one hundred degrees, the kitchen stove needed to be hotter. Opening the side door of the stove, she threw in a few more sticks of mesquite wood.

Then, reaching up into the cupboard she took down a quart-sized Mason jar of canned Elberta peaches. Her muscles strained as she twisted the tight zinc lid off the jar. Draining all of the sweet peach juice into a separate bowl, she then dumped the remaining peaches into the piecrust. From the cabinet below, tucked in a dark corner, she took out another Mason jar containing her secret ingredient. Removing the lid, she smelled the contents and then with her eyes closed, she took a big gulp of the clear liquid. It almost seemed to go up and down at the same time, leaving a burning sensation as she swallowed. The Queen poured approximately two ounces of the liquid into the bowl with the peach juice. She looked at the remaining liquid in the jar and made a mental note as to exactly how much was left. Replacing the lid tightly, the jar went back in its hiding place on the shelf below. Next, she broke two small brown eggs into a tin cup. She whisked them thoroughly before pouring them into the bowl with the peach juice. Adding ½ cup of sugar, ¼ cup flour, a teaspoon of vanilla and a pinch of salt, she whipped the mixture all together with a wooden spoon. She then poured the mix over the peaches in the pie tin. Lastly, she topped off the pie with a little fresh grated nutmeg, a sprinkle of cinnamon and a dab of butter.

After attentively weaving a fancy lattice top made from strips of dough, she then trimmed off the excess with a butcher knife. With her thumb and forefinger, she made a decorative edge on the crust giving it a ruffled appearance. She gently patted an egg glaze over the top of the piecrust so it would brown nicely in the hot oven. The Queen smiled as she admired her masterpiece. She opened the oven door and again placed her hand in the oven for a few seconds checking the temperature. Satisfied, she placed the pie on the center rack of the woodstove's oven to bake.

Just as she closed the oven door, all hell broke loose. Two of her ladies came storming into the kitchen with fists flying, screaming at each other and grabbing at each other's hair. One of the ladies grabbed the butcher knife from the baking table. Not to be outdone, the other girl grabbed a knife from the kitchen drawer. They began waving the knives, yelling curse words and threatening each other. Apparently, the dispute was over a mutual customer.

There were often fierce battles between prostitutes when it came to sharing customers. The women often fought verbally and sometimes physically. Many of the ladies were quite moody and frequently depressed enough to use *Laudanum*.

(*Laudanum was liquid opium available in drugstores for use as a painkiller/tranquilizer and many of the women became addicted to the drug after prolonged use.*)

The Queen was a very experienced businesswoman and knew how to deal with many kinds of issues. She had to be tough and yet motherly to deal with her fickle female staff. She was capable of handling just about any situation, but this one was fierce. This time, the battle became so intense that the town's sheriff had to be called down to The Cuban Queen to disarm the two young lady combatants before they actually carved each other up. Without too much trouble, the sheriff finally separated the two wildcats, disarmed them and sent them off to their rooms. The Queen thanked him for his assistance and then offered him a hot cup of coffee and a piece of her homemade peach pie fresh from the oven. The Sheriff couldn't resist. The incredible aroma of the fresh baked pie had filled the air and his mouth was already watering.

The Queen knew many disputes were settled and many favors granted over a simple piece of pie, so she worked every angle to her advantage. The halfhearted praise she gave the sheriff may have been a little artificial, but this gave her an opportunity to discuss some politics with him while he savored her delicious pie. The Sheriff raved about The Cuban Queen's pie for months to come, boasting that it was the best he had ever eaten. Of course, he had no idea the pie contained The Queen's secret ingredient, illegal moonshine whiskey.

Prohibition in Arizona went into effect on Jan. 1, 1915, five years before the national ban began. The 18th amendment made manufacturing, importing or the sale of liquor illegal in the U.S. from 1920 to 1933. Prohibition was, by most accounts, a failure and quickly produced bootleggers, speakeasies, bathtub gin and rumrunners who smuggled daily supplies of alcohol to their customers.

It was also relatively easy to find a doctor in Jerome to sign a prescription for medicinal whiskey, which could be purchased at most drugstores.

The Queen was no fool, and she knew just where to go and who to pay off to get her liquor. It was the Queen's best kept secret. She always had a steady supply of high quality moonshine that she served on a daily basis. Each week she would order several wooden cases of canned apples, cherries and peaches from the cannery.

Hidden among the jars of canned fruit were a few jars of moonshine. If one knew where to get it, a quart of 180-proof moonshine would cost about $6.50. She found that it easily sold for more than double the price she paid. Despite prohibition, The Queen made a tidy sum selling the illegal liquor during her reign in Jerome. Moonshine stills were everywhere, and revenuers were constantly on alert. Bootleggers were making moonshine in old mine tunnels, in kitchen sinks, basements, barns and even in outhouses. Police Chief John G. Crowley said that in the early spring of 1927, he and his men captured three of the most elaborate stills ever seen. Two were on Oak Creek in Sedona, and a third was on Cherry Creek just south of Jerome. The Cherry Creek still was producing over four hundred fifty gallons in one batch and was claimed to be the largest operation ever encountered in the state of Arizona.

Hidden among the jars of canned fruit were a few jars of moonshine.

This is a copper still left over from the 1920's. It was found in a crawl-space under an old house on East Ave in Jerome, Arizona.

Caught by revenuers

Chapter 11

The Luck of the Irish

John F. Ford was the Cuban Queen's star boarder.

John Francis Ford was born on September 22, 1892 in the
small western town of Cheyenne, Wyoming. Growing up,
he usually went by the name Jack and was intensely proud
of his Irish heritage. He was a very handsome fellow with
reddish brown hair and a strapping build.

It's believed his family was some of the first generation Irish to arrive on Grosse Isle, Quebec, Canada. According to the 1900 U.S. census, his father, Michael Ford, and mother, Susan Elizabeth Maley, came to the United States in the late 1850s. As a rule, the first Irish immigrants worked mostly at semi-skilled occupations. In later years, though, many of their industrious children advanced quickly and soon found themselves in management positions. Nearly fifteen percent of the entire U.S. labor force was Irish American, and by the turn of the century, about thirty percent of all of the mechanics, steel workers, plumbers, and boilermakers were of Irish decent.

Jack began working in the mines at an early age. As a young teen, he worked as a railroad brakeman for the Bingham Consolidated Mining Company in Utah. According to the *Engineering and Mining Journal*, in January of 1913, brakemen were making 22¢ an hour as long as copper prices stayed above 17¢ per pound. By the time Jack was twenty, he was making $2.00 a day for a ten-hour shift in the underground tunnels.

During the early days of mining, mules pulled heavy steel ore carts through underground tunnels. Mules were put in cages and lowered deep into the pitch-dark mineshafts where they sometimes lived their entire lives.

Because of the constant darkness, most mules became blind. Around the turn of the century, mules and ore wagons were being replaced by electric locomotives. The men sometimes called these powerful machines *electric mules*.

In 1915, Jack moved to Globe/Miami, Arizona and began working for the Inspiration Consolidated Copper Co. as a *motorman*. Early records show Jack was responsible for operating the electric motorized train that hauled the valuable ore from the tunnels to the surface. Hopes of finding gold or silver brought people to the Globe/Miami area, but it was the discovery of copper that kept them there. Copper mining was hard, dirty and dangerous work due to fires, cave-ins and explosions, but it offered great wealth and opportunity to those who came to mine.

A copy of John Francis Ford's draft card was obtained from The National Archives & Records Administration. He registered for the World War I draft in Gila County, Miami, Arizona, on June 5th, 1917 at the age of twenty-four. He listed his occupation as a motorman. A motorman is a person who operates an electrified trolley car, tram, light rail, or rapid transit train. (Wikipedia) The term is still used today.

In 1923, Jack Ford transferred from his job in Globe/Miami to the United Verde Copper Company in Jerome, Arizona. Senator Clark's United Verde Copper Mine was now one of the most modern mining operations in existence, and the miles of underground tunnels were rich in copper ore. The ore was also mixed with highly combustible sulfur deposits that often caught fire. During one of the fires, monsoon rains seeped into the hot burning mine creating steam. Pressure built up, resulting in a massive explosion that killed several men working in the tunnels.

For nearly twenty years, miles of tunnels continued to burn with seemingly no way to extinguish the inferno. It was finally determined that the only way to deal with the tunnel fires would be to dig down from above, and at the same time, create an open pit mining operation. Carrying out this plan was a colossal task. Everything on the surface above the fire including the smelter itself had to be moved. Thousands of tons of debris and rock were dug out leaving an enormous crater. As the open pit operation continued, the ore was transported by a locomotive, pulling ore cars through over a mile of newly dug tunnel called the *Hopewell Tunnel System*. The train then emerged from the mountain and continued to the newly constructed smelter in the town below called Clarkdale.

Train hauling ore in the Hopewell Tunnel

Jack quickly went to work as a *motorman* in the new Hopewell Tunnel System. He was in charge of the electric locomotive, and being experienced at the job, he was also at the upper end of the pay scale. Copper prices were soaring, and the town of Jerome and its people were prospering. Two new theaters, the Zaragoza and the Liberty Theater had opened their doors to showcase the new moving picture films. Elaborate parties and dances were being held, and gambling halls and speakeasies were opening up all over town. Everyone was making money.

Jack Ford was a happy go lucky fellow without a shy bone in his body. He loved to play pool, work hard, drink hard and was quite proficient at all three.

Jack met Annie Johnson (The Queen) at one of the local speakeasy dances. He loved to do the Irish Jig, but didn't know any of the modern dance steps. With enough liquid courage in him, however, Jack was willing to try just about anything. With a little practice, Jack and Annie soon became the couple to watch on the dance floor. He was quite smitten by her charm and beauty. She had been searching for a man with some capital of his own and someone who would compliment her own fine appearance. Jack, being the handsome Irishman he was, seemed to fit the bill perfectly. They hit it off immediately, and soon, became more than just close friends.

Playing pool and gambling in "The Billiards" in Jerome, Arizona

Jack Ford and a Hard Day's Work

It was mid-February in 1924. The whistle blew, which meant the afternoon shift was over. Jack walked up from the dark cold tunnel. He stopped for a moment to catch his breath and linger in the last few drops of sunlight. Jack took off his dirty hard hat and scratched his rusty red head while reflecting back on the day's work. He thought to himself, *No one had gotten hurt and a lot was accomplished today.* He rubbed his thick rough hands together briskly to warm them up. His fingers were cold from being in the underground tunnels for so long. The tunnels stayed at a constant fifty-eight to sixty degrees, and a man could get chilled to the bone down there.

Grabbing his lunch pail, Jack hitched a ride from the Hopewell transfer station up the hill to Jerome. He looked back over his broad shoulder at the sun setting. It was shining its last beams of light on the red rocks of the small farming community called Sedona. The sun's rays were illuminating the sculpted red rocks, making them look like they were on fire. Old man winter was quickly losing his grip on the city, and spring was fast approaching. The snow was already gone from the sunny side of Cleopatra Hill.

As he approached the town, the aroma of the evening meals lingered in the air. The Yavapai/Apache Indians on the outskirts of Jerome had their campfires blazing. As he passed the *Foreign Quarters*, he could smell the Mexicans cooking tamales, and the sound of cleaver on wood meant the numerous Chinese restaurants were vigorously chopping vegetables. After all, Jerome was a town of many ethnic groups. This mountain town was very much divided by wealth, and race. The more affluent lived high on *Cleopatra Hill,* and as you moved down in level, you also moved down in status. The red-light district was two blocks below Main Street and the foreign quarters were below that. Jack quickened his step when the familiar aroma of The Queen's southern fried chicken out-trumped all of the other smells.

The Cuban Queen Bordello was one of the nicest places in town. Jack had lived there since she first opened her doors. He climbed up the back stairs to the upper level and stopped at the communal bathroom to wash his face and comb his hair before entering  through the kitchen door. He placed his lunch pail next to the others on the floor and went in for dinner. Each morning, a lunch pail was prepared for each of her boarders. At the bottom of the tin pail was enough water for drinking and a quick hand wash. The upper tray was for sandwiches and desserts.

The Queen, with her calculating charm, and Jack, with his wit and wisdom, made the perfect team. This cunning pair would be hard to out-trump. They were soon involved in a number of other enterprises in Jerome, including a billiard hall located very near The Cuban Queen Bordello.

The place had several pool tables and a couple of faro tables. They sold cigars, Coke-a-Cola, root beer and other non-alcoholic beverages. Even though liquor was illegal, rumor had it that Jack had engineered a small copper still in a secret underground room beneath the floor and was making extra money by secretly selling moonshine. Another source of income for them was to rent out the billiard room for special events. In fact, one such event was just on the horizon.

Tomorrow would be Valentine's Day, and tonight there was a big celebration planned in the Mexican Quarter. A young Mexican couple was getting married. The Estrada-Sandoval wedding celebration and dance was being held in the billiards room. The room was all set up and the pool tables were pushed aside to make room for dancing. The celebration was just getting started and was expected to last all night. The Jerome Mexican Mariachi Band was hired for the event and was tuning up their instruments. Red paper hearts and streamers decorated the walls and all of the food was beautifully laid out. Tonight would be a big night for eating, drinking, dancing and celebrating.

Jack was in charge of keeping the receipts for the bootlegged liquor. Just in case there was any trouble, The Queen had hired Francisco Villalpando, a young Mexican man, to serve as the bouncer. Francisco's wife, Guadalupe, also worked for The Queen. Everything went off as planned, and the wedding celebration was underway. The food was excellent, the dance floor remained crowded and everyone was having a great time. As the celebration continued late into the night, an argument could be heard across the room and things started to get a little out of hand.

A Mexican man named Jose Rodriguez was quite intoxicated, became loud and kept disrupting the band. The groom, *Mr. Sandoval* asked the bouncer, *Francisco Villalpando* to escort Mr. Rodriquez out of the building. Rodriquez refused to leave and when he called Francisco's wife a *puta* (whore), heated words were exchanged. Francisco produced a gun and was heard to say that he might be using it before the night was over if Rodriquez didn't shut up and leave the dance.

It wasn't unusual in this rowdy mining town of Jerome for a brawl to break out resulting in a stabbing or even a shooting during an evening of heavy drinking. Unfortunately, this night would not be any different.

About two thirds of the homicides in Jerome involved men who had emigrated from Mexico. These people had been reared in a culture that fostered the belief that it was a man's privilege and duty to take care of his own problems without the interference of the law.

Jerome Mining News:
An article from Feb. 19, 1924

Francisco Is the Aggressor In The Fray

Early February 14th, Valentine's Day, a quarrel between Jose Rodriguez and Francisco Villalpando broke out near the Meat Market on Juarez Street about one o'clock in the morning after the Estrada-Sandoval wedding. Witnesses said Francisco was the aggressor in the fray. It was apparent that there must have been some other cause for this shooting. Six witnesses agreed that Francisco drew his gun first and shoved it against Rodriguez body. The two men were within a couple feet of each other. Just as Francisco pulled the trigger, Rodriguez swept the weapon aside with his left hand and drew his own gun and fired twice at Francisco. The first bullet cut off Francisco's little finger. The second bullet struck him squarely in the breast penetrating his heart.

The Verde Copper News reported that the jury took only a few minutes to reach a verdict of self-defense and Jose Rodriguez was acquitted.

The Villalpando's had several children. The youngest, baby Enrique was only a few months old when his father Francisco was killed in the gunfight. Francisco's wife, Guadalupe, continued to work for The Cuban Queen's bordello. Then, approximately three years later on April 29, 1927, another tragedy struck the Villalpando family.

The Verde Copper News:
An article from May 5, 1927

Five Children Left Without a Mother

Five small children were innocently plunged into a motherless world early Saturday morning around 3:30 am. A revolver in the hands of Pablino Jauriqui caused the death of Guadalupe (Apadaco) Villalpando. Witnesses in the little room next door heard the quarrel. Guadalupe claimed that Pablino Jauriqui owed her money and she called him "worthless." Three shots were fired, and it's alleged that Pablino shot Guadalupe in the head while she was still in bed. He then turned the gun on himself firing two shots in his own throat in an attempt to commit suicide.

The Verde Copper News:
An article from July 1, 1927

Jauriqui Draws a Life Sentence

Pablino Jauriqui of Jerome stood trial in the Prescott Superior Court for the murder of Guadalupe (Apadaco) Villalpando. The trial was a lengthy one. Pablino Jauriqui took the stand yesterday, the fifth day of the trial and told quietly and without any of the fire or display of temperament so usual with a person of Latino race. Pablino told the jury his story of that fatal night, still claiming it was another person, an unidentified stranger who shot and killed Guadalupe and fired two shots into his throat. After the Jury's deliberation of five hours, he was found guilty of the charge and sentenced to life in prison.

The Verde Copper News:
An article from July 1, 1927

The last page in the Spanish section

Jauaregui's Sentenciado Por La Vida
Su Declaración No Es Aspectada.

J. F. Moreno, the court's Spanish interpreter reported: Pablino Jauriqui said in Spanish, "I went to see Guadalupe; she was lying in bed in her room. We were just talking; she said I need to pay her money. I want to take her from this very bad place. Suddenly, there was a FLASH, and the sound of a gunshot." Pablino Jauriqui declared: "And I remember nothing else. I regained consciousness at the United Verde Hospital. That is where I heard Lupe had also been shot, and she was dead. I was in serious condition with two bullet wounds to my throat... I don't know who fired the gun or why they shot her. I did not do it…. I swear…check the gun. Whose gun was it? … Not mine…. Not me…. I don't know who…somebody else, I beg you… Check for yourself…please…someone…. This is not justice…. This is entrapment. You lie. Maybe you don't like Mexicans. "I did not kill my Lupe."

Both Jack Ford and The Queen were questioned about the murder of her employee, Guadalupe. Both swore they had not seen or heard anything that night.

Chapter 12
By the Light of the Moon

One Hot August Night

The lengthy murder trial of Pablino Jauriqui was held in the nearby town of Prescott, Arizona. The jury found Pablino guilty of the murder of Guadalupe (*Apadaco*) Villalpando. Even though a guilty verdict had been reached, rumors and speculation to the contrary lingered throughout Jerome. Some of the locals didn't believe Pablino committed the murder, and it seemed to most that Jack and The Queen must have known more about the incident than they were telling. Some believed The Queen either knew who pulled the trigger that night, or possibly even saw it happen. After all, during questioning she had changed her story several times regarding the evening's events. The question would seem to be; if she knew the truth and wasn't revealing it, what would be the reasoning in protecting the real killer? It's hard to say, but it was well known that client confidentiality had always been a powerful force in the prostitution business. Was there something to hide or not?

Within just a three-year period, both of the Villalpando parents, Francisco, and Guadalupe, had lost their lives to fatal gunshot wounds, and both events happened while working for The Cuban Queen. Was it just coincidence?

Unfortunately, the real victims were the five small children, two girls and three boys who were left without parents. The eldest was a pretty nine-year-old girl who had already experienced more pain than any child should. The youngest was a cute little three-year-old boy who was still too young to understand exactly what happened. The children were now the priority, and custody was quickly decided by a Prescott Superior Court judge. His decision was to keep the family together and awarded all five children to their aunt and uncle on their mother's (*Apadaco*) side of the family.

By now, The Queen had ruled in Jerome for almost a decade. During that time, the town had matured in many ways. Jerome had grown from a frontier settlement to a bustling city. Like any growing town, Jerome had its normal growing pains. The citizen's health and welfare was usually at the top of that list. Numerous health and even moral issues began to surface. Citizens were becoming tired of the lawlessness and demanded that Jerome become a place where people could feel safe and raise a family without the dangers that lurked around every corner. Because of these demands, the town of Jerome was forced to form a committee devoted solely to cleaning up gambling and prostitution.

It seemed a different Jerome was on the horizon and The Queen was starting to feel the pressure. It wasn't just the prostitution and gambling, though. It was something much more pressing and disturbing than that. The concern was something she could do nothing about, even though she had tried in the past. The problem was her race, and the simple color of her skin was now becoming a serious liability.

"The Ku Klux Klan of Yavapai Co, Prescott Ariz. Klan No. 14, and Realm of Arizona by the Exalted Cyclops" had formed a chapter in the nearby town of Prescott. Their main objective was maintaining white supremacy in Yavapai County. The Klan had been directing much of their hate tactics toward the modernism of the Jazz Era. Enforcement of prohibition was also one of their goals. They began systematically rooting out bootleggers and torching speakeasies.

The Ku Klux Klan marching on Gurley St. in Prescott, Arizona c. 1927

This inter-racial couple, a black woman and a white Irishman, selling moonshine, promoting gambling and prostitution, did not sit well with the Ku Klux Klan's agenda. While attending the murder trial of Guadalupe Villalpando in the Prescott Courthouse, The Queen heard a rumor that hooded Klansmen were advancing into Jerome, and she could possibly be one of their next targets. It was a terrifying thought for her. Not taking any chances, The Queen and her accomplice, Jack Ford quickly devised a plan.

The Queen wrote up a contract to sell The Cuban Queen Bordello to one of her working girls, a Miss Fannie Minerich. Meanwhile, Jack cashed his last paycheck and began packing his 1926 Nash Ambassador.

*Arizona Yavapai County records confirm that in 1927 a Mrs.
Fannie Minerich purchased lot 2 and a part of lot 3 in Block 14,
together with a two-story twelve-hundred square foot building and all
improvements on 300 Rich Street for the sum of five-hundred dollars.
The building known as The Cuban Queen Bordello was later given
the address of "324 Queen Street."*

Photo circa 1950's

*The Cuban Queen Bordello building is in the upper left of this photo.
The concrete building in the foreground is the Jail House. What's left
of the jail still remains and is now a tourist attraction known as
"The Sliding Jail."*

Jack and The Queen's plan was to clean out their bank accounts and then slip out of town in the middle of the night. Countless thoughts were spinning around in The Queen's head. At times, she had thoughts of quitting her profession altogether, settling down and maybe even having a real family. Regrettably though, these were only empty thoughts. Having children was no longer an option due to her age and health complications created from her many years of infidelity. The Queen reflected back on the baby daughter she had abandoned twenty-five years ago so she could become a sporting lady. It saddened her to think of spending the rest of her life childless. However, unbeknownst to anyone, she had devised a plan to fix that also.

The Queen always had a special fondness for the Villalpando's youngest child. He was baptized just a few months after his father Francisco was gunned down. In fact, records show that The Queen was at the baptism and even signed the document. The young boy, *Enrique Villalpando* was born August 3, 1923, and was baptized in the Holy Family Parish in Jerome on December 11, 1924. Her signature appears on that document as *Anita Gonzales* one of her many aliases.

It was August 3, 1927, and little Enrique Villalpando was now turning four years old. For his birthday, The Queen prearranged for him to spend the night and then took the little boy to *Hoyt's Ye Olde Candy Shoppe* for a sack of hard candy. But her generosity didn't stop there. She stopped at the *Jerome Mercantile* where they sold dry goods and children's clothing. The Queen outfitted Enrique with several pair of knee-length knickers with the button closures, a few shirts, socks, a pair of canvas shoes and a sturdy pair of lace up leather high-tops. The storekeeper was astonished by the amount of money she spent on the little boy. He seemed a little puzzled when she then laid a heavy wool tweed outer jacket on the counter. After all, it was the middle of August, the hottest month of the year. Handsomely dressed in his new sailor themed garments and holding his new toy bear, little Enrique could have been the boy in a Norman Rockwell painting for the Saturday Evening Post. When they arrived home, Enrique fell asleep, exhausted from the day of eating candy and trying on clothes. While the boy slept, The Queen filled a picnic basket full of cold fried chicken, baking powder biscuits and several pieces of fruit. It was enough food to last someone for several days. Gathering Enrique's new gifts and the rest of her personal belongings, she put everything into a large suitcase.

For the past couple of days, Jack had been carefully sorting and packing things into the car, including an extra can of gas and a second spare tire. He even found space (against his better judgment) for The Queen's prized rosebush. She had insisted earlier that he dig it up and take it with them. The Queen had purchased the prized rosebush from the Hansohn's Company, a variety store in Jerome.

For some reason, the rosebush had a special place in her heart. She had planted it near the front door of the bordello and against all odds, kept it alive, watering it daily with her dishwater. It was quite a chore protecting it from the ravaging appetites of the donkeys that were used to deliver groceries and firewood by day, and were turned loose at night. The fragrant roses were sweet and intense, certainly a contrast from the toxic fumes so prevalent in Jerome.

The Queen had always lived her life above the law and usually took what she wanted regardless of whom it might affect. Therefore, keeping in character she carried the sleeping little boy to their car and with everything packed and securely tied down, the threesome disappeared that hot August moonlit night without a trace.

Heading northwest and wanting to put some distance between them and Jerome, The Queen encouraged Jack to pick up the pace. In the back of his mind however, he knew he needed to navigate the bone-jarring dirt road with care. The car was packed to the gills and the last thing he needed was for things to shift and fall off the car in the middle of the night. The bandits hoped to slip out of town undetected and be miles away before anyone even realized they were gone. Jack wanted to be out of Arizona and into Nevada before daybreak.

Jack had been behind the wheel, driving for more than 16 hours. The mid morning temperatures were quickly rising and the car was starting to overheat.

The breeze from the open windows provided little comfort to the restless baby boy now wedged in amongst The Queen's belongings in the backseat. *(Any type of air conditioning for automobiles was unheard of until almost a decade later.)* Jack had lived in the desert long enough to know to avoid the daytime heat. Even the animals would burrow beneath the surface or hide in the shade during the day. Cactus would even wait until the cool of the night to reveal their flowers. The notorious *Death Valley* would be the next leg of their getaway. Jack knew his 1926 Nash was no match for the unrelenting heat at *Furnace Creek* where it had been known to reach over one hundred thirty degrees in August. Getting through the desert at night was definitely their only option.

Jack needed to get some rest, so he parked the car under a large mesquite tree, just out of sight of the main road. The Queen took off the boy's shoes and stripped him down to his underwear. He played in the desert sand while she made lunch for the three of them. Suddenly, the silence of the desert was broken by a blood curdling scream. The barefoot child had stepped on a scorpion and now had a nasty sting just below the ankle. Jumping to the rescue, The Queen snatched up the boy and laid him on a blanket. With her heart pounding and wondering "What next" she started having second thoughts and began questioning her motivations for even taking the boy. Was it really worth all the trouble? Was she even the motherly type? It quickly occurred to her that it really didn't matter anyway. It was too late, and there was no turning back now. Soon the child was in extreme pain and burning with fever. She calmed him by cooling him off with a wet cloth. As she looked down at the helpless child, she made a promise to herself to amend her lifestyle and become a good mother to this young boy. It was at that moment that she decided to rename the boy *Henry Ford*. She promised herself that from that point on, she would provide him with the best life she possibly could. The new family would lay low in the shade and try to get some sleep before resuming their journey by night. If they made it through the desert, the plan was to drive west across California, and then follow the coastline north to Oregon, Washington, and finally into Canada.

Back in Jerome, Guadalupe (Apadaco) Villalpando's family wondered why the woman that ran the boarding house had not returned young Enrique. Sick with worry, they waited, but their hopes grew thin. The woman and the boy had just disappeared. After a few days, they reported their suspicions to the authorities. Speaking only Spanish, it became quite difficult for the Villalpando family to obtain any information, especially when no one even knew the Cuban Queen's real name. To some, the police department's attitude toward the grieving family was very cut and dried and no formal investigation was ever carried out. Some say, the reason was simply racial and the boy was thought of as just another missing Mexican. The family would just have to look for the boy on their own.

Chapter 13

Camping in Canyonville

Camping in Canyonville, Oregon

Jack, The Queen and the little boy had been on the road for nearly a week and most of the trip seemed to bring nothing but trouble. The weight of the luggage and the rough dirt roads had been too much for the old tires on the car. As a result, they were cursed with a number of flats. The little boy recovered from his scorpion encounter, but was now fidgety and tired of being cooped up in a blistering hot car. On top of that, he was confused, and rightfully so, as he continued to cry for his mother. The boy also missed his siblings, especially his older brother, Raul. Back in Jerome, the boy's family spoke only Spanish. The Queen tried to comfort him, but Enrique just didn't understand the English she and Jack were speaking. Jack's nerves were now stretched as thin as the bald tires on the Nash.

Days later they finally made it into Oregon, and the cooler weather was a welcomed relief. Jack stopped in a small town called Canyonville and ordered two new tires for the car. They rented a tiny cabin at a nearby campground on the South Umpqua River. The three of them stayed there for several days waiting for the tires to arrive. Little Enrique finally settled down and enjoyed playing in the campground. Jack assessed the load situation and was determined to lighten things before going on to Canada. He insisted The Queen toss out a few things including what he called, "that damned rosebush." The thorns had pricked him every time he needed to dig around to get something. The Queen reluctantly gave in and decided she would plant her dying rosebush there in the Oregon campground. As soon as the new tires arrived, they continued on their journey north. They drove for about thirty minutes when all of a sudden The Queen demanded that Jack stop, turn around and go back. She said she had a vision that they were to live there in Canyonville, Oregon, and not Canada. Jack knew her well enough not to go against her so-called "voodoo visions", so he turned the car around and went back to the campground.

The returning tenants were well liked by the owners, and were happy to see them back. To the couple's surprise, they were even offered the job of campground manager. The owners had actually been in the market to sell their business, and within a few months, The Queen was able to secure a five-year lease with an option to buy the entire campground property. Jack and The Queen were thrilled. They were also very cautious not to put their true names on any public documents for fear of being found. They changed their identities and never mentioned a word to anyone about their lives back in Arizona. Jack and The Queen were only known to the people of Canyonville as Mr. and Mrs. Ford and their son Henry. Life there seemed to be quite agreeable for the new Ford family. They soon turned the main house, which sat right on the highway, into a restaurant and gas station and simply named it FORD'S.

FORD'S on Hwy 99 in Canyonville, Oregon

They continued to manage the campground and eight small cabins. The property later became quite a tourist attraction and even included a variety of animals. There were peacocks, deer, and even a caged bear and a mountain lion. They also kept a pet monkey that is said to have preferred Jack's beer rather than a banana.

J. F. Ford was still a happy-go-lucky person and the local Oregonians enjoyed listening to his tall tales. Of course, Mrs. Ford (The Queen) was all business and made sure everything ran like a Swiss watch. Jack Ford, now going by the name of J. F. Ford, established and ran the gas station selling gasoline under an agreement with the Standard Oil Company of California.

Pumping gas at Ford's Gas Station

The restaurant business worked out perfectly for The Queen. Of course, the few employees at the Ford Café also knew her only as Mrs. Ford. Later describing her, they said Mrs. Ford certainly wasn't one to spare the make-up. She wore a lot of jewelry, especially diamonds, and often dressed in elaborate clothing with a modern flare. They claimed the woman had a rigid personality, was quite self-centered and didn't have many close friends. They also stated that she had definite ideas about how she wanted things done and was very tight with money. The Ford Café had a pleasant atmosphere and became very successful. To help draw people into their restaurant, The Ford's put up billboards on Highway 99 for fifty miles in each direction.

The Queen was an excellent cook as well as a fine host. Hungry diners would travel considerable distances to enjoy her fine cooking. Her fried chicken was a favorite. Most of her fryers were raised locally and her fried chicken recipe was simple. She soaked the cut-up chicken overnight in a solution of water, salt and just a little sugar. Then, draning off the water, the chicken pieces were dusted with finely ground cornmeal and wheat flour and cooked in hot grease in a large cast-iron skillet. She always made her famous baking-powder biscuits and pie dough from scratch using lard. Her homemade blackberry and peach pie topped with fresh whipped cream were served regularly for desserts.

The height of The Queen's success came in 1946 when *Duncan Hines* gave the Ford Café mention in their very popular magazine called, *Adventures in Good Eating.*

The magazine featured her southern fried chicken, baking powder biscuits, her famous peach pie and several other specialties. It's not known whether her peach pie contained her secret ingredient!

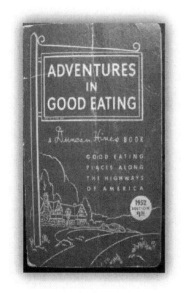

From the late 1930s, Duncan Hines was known as America's first national restaurant critic. The Adventures in Good Eating guidebook pointed travelers to the best restaurants, motels, and vacation destinations. With the popularity of these guidebooks and the strength of the Hines' reputation, Duncan Hines almost single-handedly transformed the entire U.S. Hospitality industry.

The Fords were a hard-working family and were well respected by the local Oregon community. The people of Canyonville never suspected that the boy Mr. and Mrs. Ford called Henry was not their own child and Henry was too young at the time to have ever known he had been abducted. He always thought The Queen was his natural mother and had no reason to believe otherwise. It all seemed perfectly normal since The Queen claimed to be part Mexican.

Twelve-year-old 7ᵗʰ grader, Henry Ford, (Enrique Villalpando) is the boy on the left standing next to his teacher in Canyonville, Oregon, c.1936

As Henry grew into a charming young man, he helped out in the café bussing tables, washing dishes and cooking. For extra spending money, he would also work outside pumping gas and washing windshields.

Henry grew up as a somewhat pampered child. He always had a charming personality and was well liked in school. He grew up and went on to attend the University of Oregon. The locals remembered how he loved to drive fast cars and how popular he was with the young girls. It wasn't long before Henry found that special young woman and married. The new couple soon started a family of their own. Their first child was a boy they named Mike. Henry and his wife continued to work in the Ford Café, and with The Queen's coaching, Henry became an excellent cook himself. The Fords ran their very successful operation for the next twenty years.

Henry Ford holding new baby boy, Mike. Notice "Ford Café" on his chef's hat.

Anita Ford, (The Queen) and Jack Ford are on the left.
Henry Ford is the boy on the right, Canyonville, Oregon. c. 1940's

The Queen, with her cunning ways, continued living her secret life in Canyonville, Oregon. Even though the Ford Café had a telephone, she would often go down to the phone company's office to use the only public phone in town. She was secretly keeping in touch with her natural daughter, Hattie Seymour, with her brothers, and even her old friend and ex-husband, Jelly Roll Morton.

Jelly Roll was not showing the resiliency The Queen had shown. He had not weathered the storm of the great depression like some. Times were tough for him, and his health was in a downward spiral. He decided to swallow what pride he had left and telephoned his old friend and ex-wife, Anita. Jelly Roll was in need of a big favor...and that favor was money.

Chapter 14

Jelly's in a Jam

Jelly Roll Morton hit hard times and sold all of his jewelry,
except the diamond in his front tooth.

In 1927, Jelly Roll Morton married a showgirl named Mable Bertrand. They lived together in New York for about twelve years. With the great depression of the 1930s and the near collapse of the record companies, Jelly's contracts were not renewed. Both he and his music slowly faded into obscurity. Jelly Roll Morton reached the height of his popularity between 1925 and 1929, but now his jazz music was out of style. In its place, the Big Band sound had become the dominant force in music.

The older generation of musicians realized that no one was interested in listening to the old style jazz tunes anymore. There was no longer a market for small-band recordings, and recording companies were extremely reluctant to take any risks. Some musicians like Earl Hines and Louis Armstrong financed their own big bands, while others like Jelly Roll Morton and King Oliver faded into the shadows.

Jelly Roll's jazz style was outdated and he was now being upstaged by younger artists. The music industry was still playing his songs on the radio, but various artists were now rearranging them and taking all the credit. If Jelly Roll would have had the proper paperwork in place, he would have been receiving royalties from these recordings and certainly would have become a millionaire. Certain people had taken advantage of Jelly over the years and during that time, racial prejudice had played a large part in his musical demise.

In February 1940, Jelly Roll got word that his Godmother Laura Hunter (Echo) was gravely ill and didn't have much time left. Echo and her husband, Ed Hunter, were now living in California. Ed was getting on in years and being completely blind, he needed help making Echo's final arrangements. Jelly Roll felt terrible and wanted to help, but he was so broke that he couldn't afford to make the trip from New York to California. With no other family to help out, in his desperation he contacted The Queen and asked her to help take care of his godmother's funeral.

The Queen, now living in Oregon, was hesitant but agreed to the task. She drove to Los Angeles and stayed with her brother Dink Johnson while taking care of all the details. It seems that one of those details had included going through Echo's personal belongings. It was alleged that during the process, she helped herself to a few things including Echo's jewerly box, which contained all of Echo's expensive rings and diamond jewelry. When Jelly Roll asked The Queen if his godmother had left anything of value, The Queen claimed everything was already gone when she got there. Jelly Roll felt awful that he couldn't make it to his godmother's funeral.

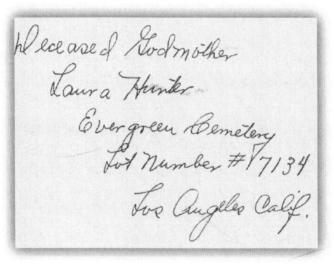

In The Queen's own handwriting, a note was found with Jelly Roll's Godmother's, Laura Hunter (Echo) burial information. Laura died February 14, 1940.

The world's pressures were closing in on Jelly Roll and his health was deteriorating fast. Doctors had advised him that his heart was failing and that he needed to slow down. But how could he? Throughout the 1930s his music was being broadcast by hundreds of radio stations to millions of people. You couldn't turn on the radio without hearing one of Jelly Roll's songs. He was fighting an uphill battle to receive any royalties from the musical compositions he had published, but without money, it was next to impossible to carry on the legal battle.

Below is an excerpt from a 1940 "Downbeat" magazine.

```
Oct 1, 1940:

"I have been robbed by the American Music
Recorders and swindled out of millions…. Everyone
is playing my stuff, and I don't even get credit.
Kansas City Style, Chicago Style, New Orleans
Style, Hell, they're all my styles. I wrote that
music!..........Jelly Roll Morton
```

Jelly's health was declining, his music was out-dated and he realized that the only way he could survive was to make some sort of musical comeback. He had already sold all of his diamonds except the one imbedded in his front tooth. He was so broke he couldn't even get his clothing out of the dry cleaners.

Jelly Roll certainly wasn't accustomed to asking anyone for favors, especially money. For the past decade, Jelly's pockets were always lined with cash, but these were different times. As tough as it was for him, he swallowed his pride and again contacted The Queen. Jelly explained to her that if he just had money to hire legal counsel, he would be able to collect on his royalties. He made it very clear that surely he would be worth millions. The word millions" was all that The Queen needed to hear. She talked it over with her husband, Jack, whom she had been married to for the past sixteen years. With Jack's approval, they jointly agreed to lend Jelly Roll the bankroll he needed. The loan however, would come with certain conditions. The Queen wired Jelly a partial payment for traveling money and invited him to come out to Canyonville, Oregon to finalize all of the details. Jelly agreed and began planning for a long trip across country.

Jelly's Last Roll

The day the money arrived, Jelly Roll was feeling very optimistic and started packing up everything he owned and putting it all into his two cars. Jelly Roll's heart was weak and each breath was labored. His wife Mable, or "May" as Jelly Roll called her, helped him pack his latest manuscripts, his records and what was left of his fancy suits into his black 1938 Cadillac. He then hitched the "Caddy" to the back of his Lincoln and was ready to hit the road. Jelly Roll's final journey out west began in the late fall of 1940. It was shortly after his fiftieth birthday, which fell on October 20th.

Naturally, his wife May was quite worried about him, but she also knew Jelly Roll was a stubborn man. Once he had his mind made up, no one could stop him, not even her. May held her tears at bay while she made Jelly a pot of hot coffee and poured it into his thermos for the long trip. In her heart, May knew this possibly could be the last time she would ever see him. Not once, however, did she let her fear show. She knew Jelly needed her support now more than ever. Jelly Roll encouraged May not to worry about anything and promised that he was going to find work and make his return to fame. He assured her everything was going to be alright.

May never suspected a thing even though Jelly had been lying to her the whole time. He had been telling May that his godmother, Echo, was sick and that he needed to be there for her last days. In reality, Echo had been dead and buried for at least nine months. He told May that after he put his godmother to rest, he was going to get a new band together in California where the weather was warmer and the pastures were greener. He promised May he would write to her often and send her money soon. Kissing May goodbye, Jelly slid behind the wheel of his Lincoln, adjusted the seat and mirrors and drove off into the late afternoon sun. In the back of her mind, May wondered how he was going to make the trip without any money. He never once mentioned a word to her about The Queen or their planned meeting. Once on the road, Jelly didn't drive southwest toward sunny California. Instead, he headed northwest into the cold. Of course, he was heading for Canyonville, Oregon, to see The Queen.

It must have been quite unnerving for a feeble man with a weak heart to travel all the way across the country with winter coming on. He was driving one car and towing another, staying in cheap hotels and in Catholic churches, and sometimes even sleeping in the car. The once famous Jelly Roll Morton stopped at a few places along the way asking for work, but unfortunately there were no takers. It seemed no one wanted to hear a washed up old man with old fashion clothes and out-dated music. Jelly Roll was now a stranger in most of the towns where twenty years earlier he had been a sensation. At each stop, he would try to look up old friends, but they had all moved away. His own family didn't even want to see "him and his underworld ways." Jelly Roll had been on the road for almost two weeks. The temperatures had been in the fifties and sixties and most of the Midwest had enjoyed an Indian summer. Parts of Iowa had been unusually warm for that time of year, but things were about to change. At 7:30 AM on the 11th of November 1940, the weather forecast on his car radio reported: *"Chicago fifty-five degrees, Davenport checked in with fifty-four. On the other side of Iowa, however, Sioux City's temperature is only twelve degrees."*

Jelly continued to drive, disregarding the weather reports. Temperatures dropped sharply, winds picked up, then rain followed by sleet and heavy snow began to fall. The windshield wipers slapped out a steady rhythm on the icy windshield, while he hummed a new tune in his head. The Lincoln's heater was on full blast but his thin frail body was still chilled to the bone. He squinted through a clear spot in the frosted windshield at the unfamiliar landscape. The blinding snow seemed to be moving horizontally. He was completely exhausted and almost felt as if he was in some sort of trance. The car radio warned, *"The storm is big; expect freezing temperatures, gusting winds and heavy snow. Extreme blizzard conditions are likely. The cold snow will be soft and powdery, and will cover much of Iowa, starting with the southwestern part of the state tonight and tomorrow, hitting the Midwest and spreading north and east from there."*

The Newspaper reported: Nov 13, 1940

16.8 inches of snow fell in 24 hours and 154 deaths are blamed on the blizzard

November 11, Armistice Day, the blizzard temperatures suddenly plunged from the 60s to zero, winds gusted to 32 mph and 16.8 inches of snow fell in 24 hours. In South Dakota, the storm brought up to **27 inches** of snow to some locations. Along the Mississippi River several hundred duck hunters had taken time off from work and school to take advantage of the ideal hunting conditions. Weather forecasters had not predicted the severity of the oncoming storm; as a result, many of the hunters were not dressed for cold weather. When the storm began, many hunters took shelter on small islands in the Mississippi River, and the 50 mph (80 km/h) winds and 5-foot (1.5 m) waves overcame their encampments. Some became stranded on the islands and then froze to death in the single-digit temperatures that moved in overnight. Others tried to make it to shore and drowned. Duck hunters constituted about half of the **49 deaths** in Minnesota. The storm claimed **5 vessels, and 66 lives** on Lake Michigan. **The storm is the worst in recorded history.**

The authorities encouraged motorists to stay home and off the roads. Jelly Roll could barely make out the highway in front of him and yet defiantly and foolishly kept on driving.

Jelly Roll slipped off the road and banged up the cars in that horrible snowstorm. He was fortunate not to have gotten hurt, but was forced to have the Cadillac towed and stored somewhere in Montpelier, Idaho, before continuing on his journey.

Armistice Day Blizzard on Nov.11, 1940

As he drove the lonely miles across the country, his mind wandered. He recalled the time when he felt he was on top of the world. He was *The Piano Professor*, *The King of Jazz* and the most popular musician around.

He remembered that the beautiful young women called *Jazzebells* loved to follow his shows as he toured. There was a time when he wore a different suit every day and always had a big roll of cash stuffed in his pocket. He wore diamonds on every finger and even had diamonds pinned to his underwear for safekeeping. Inside his suit jacket, he would always carry a pearl-handled pistol. He grinned, as he thought back on his wild younger days when he was married to Anita. Jelly pulled the rearview mirror down and looked at the diamond still embedded in his front tooth. It was the very one she had given him as a wedding gift back in 1919. His grin quickly faded as he took a good look at himself, almost horrified as to how terrible he looked. The reflection looking back at him was a scrawny old man with sunken cheeks, a rutted face, thin gray hair and whiskers. He looked like a man twice his age. Scratching at his unshaven jaw, he contemplated whether to shave or maybe grow a beard to hide his aged face.

In one of Jelly Roll's earlier interviews, he said, *"Mama-Nita* (that's what he lovingly called The Queen) *was devoted to me. She respected me when we were married like few women do these days. She was a very beautiful woman and always dressed very attractively with plenty of diamonds to elaborate her style. I could have not wished for a finer woman than Mama-Nita. I miss her terribly. I made a big mistake by leaving her, but nevertheless it happened. Those days with her were the best years of my life. Days full of sunshine, diamonds, music and sweet Anita sitting by my side as we traveled up and down the west coast in our brand new motor car making music."*

On Nov. 13, 1940, with his destination almost in sight, Jelly Roll stopped to spend the night at Scotty's Gas Station and Auto Camp near John Day, Oregon. While there, he wrote a letter to his wife, May, back in New York detailing his trip and the horrifying events of the storm he had endured. He slid the letter in an envelope and laid it on the nightstand next to the bed. He would mail it in the morning. Jelly looked at his watch. It was getting late and he was beat. If everything went as planned, he only had about eight hours of driving time before he would be in Canyonville, Oregon.

Jelly glanced at himself in the mirror across the room. He wondered what Anita might think when she saw him. He wondered if she had kept her beauty. It had been eighteen years since they had seen each other. In the morning, he planned to take a bath, shave and dress in his very best clothes, but for now, he just needed a good night's sleep.

Chapter 15

She Sold His Soul to Satan

*Jelly Roll's godmother, Eulalie He'caud, aka Echo Hunter,
was a prominent French-speaking Voodoo Priestess.*

Jelly Roll just could not seem to warm up. The strange bed
was uncomfortable and for as tired as he was, he had
gotten very little sleep. All night long he tossed and turned
as hundreds of thoughts swirled around in his head. His
recollections took him back to when he was just a young
teenager and went to stay with his godmother. Echo was
never a particularly handsome woman, but she was very
intelligent. She wore rings on every finger and always
seemed to have plenty of money. He recalled the strange

voodoo ceremony she had performed that day many years ago. Echo looked into her crystal ball and predicted he would become a famous musician, but not without great sacrifice. He always believed his godmother had sold his soul to Satan as a ransom for his musical talent. He wondered how his life would have turned out had it not been for music. Perhaps his recent acceptance of the Catholic faith and denouncing voodoo had something to do with his failing heart. Jelly had never been much of a spiritual person. It was actually his wife, Mable, who had encouraged him to accept Catholicism. Jelly kept worrying about Mable and how she was doing back in New York. He knew he needed to send her money so she could pay on all the bills he left behind. The financial help from his old friend and ex-wife Anita was simply his last hope. His continued survival depended on a musical comeback. It was that simple.

By the next morning, the cold mountain town of John Day, Oregon was well below freezing. Still feeling tired, Jelly dressed in his best clothes and returned the room key. He filled the car with gas, hastily scraped the ice from the windshield and got into the driver's seat. Traveling would now be faster without the Cadillac in-tow. This was the last leg of his journey and if all went well, he would be in Canyonville, Oregon before nightfall.

Jelly Roll knew he was not well. The hard, fast life he always loved had certainly taken its toll. He knew that his days remaining on this earth were numbered. Some say his chronic ill health was due to a knife wound he received while playing in a Washington nightclub. A rowdy patron attacked Jelly Roll, stabbing him in the chest and he never fully recovered from that injury. Others speculate that an undiagnosed case of syphilis could very well have been the cause of his failing health. Back in Jelly's wilder days, he had contracted something called *Whores Itch* causing a large patch of sores to form around his groin. He would constantly scratch until he became poisoned with infection. He claimed to be cured by a voodoo chant and a concoction made from sulfur, lard and bluestone, *(an old astringent and remedy for canker sores.)*

Jelly had been both flat broke and flush with money a number of times in his roller coaster life. He had experienced everything from fame and fortune, to poverty and depression. Somehow, though, he had managed to hold-on to his trademark thirty-point diamond that The Queen had given him years ago as a wedding gift. Jelly Roll always swore he would never part with the diamond in his front tooth and vowed to take it with him to his grave.

After weeks on the road, Jelly Roll finally made it to Canyonville, Oregon. After all of his anxious anticipation, the reunion turned out to be quite uneventful and even a little uncomfortable while the main focus was to work out the terms and details of his loan. He soon found out that the main clause in the loan contract declared that The

Queen would become partners in any future recordings Jelly might produce. Jelly didn't like the idea much, but in his desperation, he agreed to the terms. Jelly offered to let Jack and The Queen hold his diamond for collateral, but after some discussion, they all agreed that if he were to make a return to the music world, Jelly Roll would need to look the part of the dazzling showman he always was. After all, the diamond had always been Jelly's trademark. Jelly Roll would keep the diamond and wear it for now. The deal was done.

The Queen immediately started managing Jelly as she had always done in the past. She also sensed the jealous tension between her husband Jack and Jelly Roll. Knowing that Jelly would not be received well in Oregon, a quick call was made to her brother, Dink Johnson and arrangements were made for Jelly to stay with Dink and his wife, Stella in Los Angeles.

Jelly Roll knew that if he was going to make his return to music he would need the big band sound that was now popular. For the past several years, he had diligently been writing scores intended for a big orchestra with twelve to twenty musicians. He hoped to put together a group of four or five trumpet players, several saxophones, a couple of trombones, a rhythm section and some strings. But getting a band of that size together to practice the new numbers was a challenge that would soon prove to be futile.

Even though his spirits were high and he was eager to show off his new compositions, Jelly was only able to pull together a small band of barely six musicians. The new band included Kid Ory on trombone, Pee Wee Brice on trumpet, a guitarist, a bass player and Dink, The Queen's brother as the drummer. Jelly Roll knew very well that a big band sound is arranged in advance and noted precisely on sheet music. Unfortunately, several of his new band members couldn't read music and played strictly by ear. Jelly tried repeatedly to teach his new band members their parts by first playing them on the piano, but it just didn't work. His patience soon grew thin and simply did not have the energy to continue. Musically, the new band was a disaster and as a result, they never played anywhere in public. Jelly Roll was growing weaker by the day and even if the new band would have worked out, he wouldn't have had the endurance to play the all-night clubs like in the old days. He hardly had enough energy to sit at the piano for just an hour at a time.

The Queen recalled the last time she heard Jelly Roll play:

"The last time I heard him play, he played a new piece he wrote called 'Sweet Substitute.' Ferddy looked shockingly feeble, sick, old, and even a little angry. He wore his old southern-gentleman's suit with dignity and when he smiled, the diamond in his tooth still glistened. Anyone that knew him could tell that something was wrong."

The Queen made a few trips from Oregon to California to visit her brother Dink and to check on Jelly Roll Morton's progress. After all, she now had a stake in his success. Unfortunately, though, the news was not good.

It had only been six months since Jelly Roll left New York, and already he was realizing the cold, hard truth. Putting a big band together was next to impossible in his weakened condition. He was also suffering from bouts of depression. Anita learned of Jelly Roll's trials and could see for herself how his health had deteriorated. During one of her visits in late June, Jelly asked her to take him to the hospital. After talking to the doctor, she realized the severity of his condition. Jelly Roll Morton was fighting a losing battle and didn't have much longer to live.

On July 10, 1941 The Queen, noticeably shaken, phoned her husband Jack with the sad news. Jelly Roll Morton had succumbed to heart failure and died in her arms at 2:00 p.m. in the L.A. County Hospital. Jack immediately left their eighteen-year-old son Henry Ford in charge of running their operation in Canyonville and flew to Los Angeles to comfort his wife. When Jack arrived at the airport, The Queen picked him up in Jelly Roll's Lincoln and drove straight to a nearby motel where they sat and talked. All Jack seemed to be concerned about was the money that they had loaned Jelly Roll. The Queen instructed Jack to just lay low and not to even attend the service. She calmly told Jack not to worry about the money and assured him everything was under control.

The Queen made Jelly Roll's final arrangements. Jelly Roll Morton's body was prepared and was resting peacefully in his coffin at the funeral parlor. He was dressed in his finest pinstriped suit with a stylish fedora sitting comfortably on his head. His trademark diamond, set in gold in his front tooth was still in place just as he always wanted. His lips were deliberately sealed slightly apart with mortician's wax, just enough to expose the sparkle of the diamond. Additionally, Jelly's pallbearers would be a few of his old jazz musician friends. Everything was arranged and his last wishes seemed to have been fulfilled.

The very next day, however, when the coffin lid was raised for the viewers in the parlor, something unbelievably sinister had taken place. Jelly Roll's lips had been pried wide open with what looked like a pocketknife. The diamond was gone, leaving an ugly, gaping, black hole in his tooth where the jewel had been. The thirty-point trademark diamond that he wished to be buried with had been stolen. Although impractical as it may seem to bury such an expensive gem, it was Jelly Roll's lifelong desire to be buried with it in place.

When The Queen was questioned, she seemed quite shocked and adamantly denied knowing anything about the horrific theft. Who then was the scoundrel who had crept into the undertaker's parlor during the middle of the night and pried the diamond from Jelly's front tooth? Now America's first great jazz composer, Jelly Roll Morton, must be laid to rest, violated with his lips forever pried apart exposing a horrible gaping hole where his trademark diamond once sparkled.

Among all the confusion, the funeral director quickly lowered the lid and made the decision to have a closed casket service. This would at least spare the viewers the awful sight and retain Jelly Roll's dignity during his final passage.

STATE OF CALIFORNIA
CERTIFICATION OF VITAL RECORD

STATE OF CALIFORNIA
DEPARTMENT OF HEALTH SERVICES

The Queen, now posing as Jelly Roll's widow signed his death certificate on July 14th. His funeral service was at the historic Saint Patrick's Church, followed by his burial at Calvary Catholic Cemetery in Los Angeles on July 16th, 1941.

During the service, The Queen spoke emotionally to anyone who cared to listen of Jelly Roll's decline and death. *"I took care of Ferd during his terrible illness and his last days on earth. He expired in my arms."* She sobbed and wiped away tears. *"His heart just couldn't take it anymore. Ferddy was a tough, stubborn man and he would have never asked to be taken to a hospital unless he was in a very bad way. He begged me to keep anointing his lips with oil that was blessed by a New York Bishop. Ferddy came back to me when he knew his time was short. I was the only woman he ever truly loved."*

Less than one hundred people attended the service. Jelly Roll's pallbearers were musicians including Papa Mutt Carey, Ed Garland, Kid Ory, Fred Washington, Spencer Johnson, Frank Whither and Paul Howard. It was reported that Reb Spikes, Jelly's old song writing partner, hitched a ride and just made it to the cemetery in time. A small number of musicians were going to put a brass band together and play for the occasion, but the church officials said they would not allow "such a display." Most said, Jelly would have loved that.

A catholic priest named Father Perez, who Jelly Roll had never even met, performed the service and celebrated a *Requiem High Mass.* The service and last rites recited over the famed piano player, composer and contributor to the world of jazz was short and pointed. A few people sent telegraphs, others telephoned and a few sent flowers. After the funeral, a small procession wound its way through the grassy hillsides of sunny California to the cemetery.

2 Don Redman   1 Jelly Roll Morton
3 Teddy Hill
4 Sammy Stuart
5 Hot Lips Page
6 Edgar Hayes
7 Fess Williams
8 Manny Logan
9 Wm. Braud
10 Henry (Red) Allen
11 Cliff Jackson
12 Bardu Ali
13 Bobby Hargraves
14 Eddie Barefield
15 Oscar Hogan
16 Billy Butler
17 Clarence Moore
18 Maurice Hubert
19 Ace Prince
20 Mercer Ellington
21 Henry Wells
22 Jimmie Gorham – Phila 703 Broad st
23. Pancho Diggs. Newark. Statesland.
24 Louis Mitchell
25 Perry Nixon

This is a copy of the sign-in guest register for those that attended Jelly Roll Morton's funeral on July 19, 1941. These are the first twenty-five entries.

Standing at Jelly Roll Morton's Grave

The Queen seemed to take the whole affair extremely hard, especially at the cemetery. After the casket was lowered into the ground, the pallbearers along with a couple other musicians tossed a few shovels full of dirt on top of the casket and merely walked away. For the most part the entire affair was quite unemotional.

The Queen was now standing alone at Jelly Roll's open grave in her tight black wool skirt and short wool jacket. She was rather uncomfortable in the hot California midday sun. Her new high-heeled shoes sunk deep into the soft grass. With tear-filled eyes, she looked through her veil at the fresh dirt on top of Jelly's casket.

It was now final. Her eyes descended to her folded hands. She noticed the age spots and how old and abused they looked. Her hands told the truth even if her lips did not. For her entire life, she had lied about her age. Even her own husband Jack didn't know she was ten years older than she claimed to be. She thought to herself, "Doesn't every woman lie about her age?" All the hard work of scrubbing pots and pans, mopping floors, kneading bread and cutting up chicken had taken its toll. She once called herself *The Cuban Queen,* but most of her life was more reminiscent of a slave's life.

Anita twisted at the diamond rings on her fingers. She knew some of them were stolen from Jelly Roll's godmother Echo, but it didn't bother her in the least. She never did like Jelly Roll's godmother. In fact, she hated the woman.

The Queen had always been jealous of Jelly's and Echo's relationship. She always feared Echo to some extent because of her voodoo, but at the same time she also respected her.

She was still a little bitter about having to deal with Echo's passing. After all, she only agreed to help because it was Jelly's godmother. When all of the arrangements were taken care of, she felt she deserved some sort of compensation, so she simply helped herself to Echo's jewelry. She always believed her thievery was perfectly warranted. With each recollection, she seemed to find some sort of twisted validation for her actions and misgivings.

One thing The Queen did regret, was letting Pablino Jauriqui take the fall for the murder of Henry's mother Guadalupe Villalpando. On the morning of the crime, she recalled seeing a prominent man of Jerome, who was also a regular client of Guadalupe's, leave The Cuban Queen Bordello. She remembered seeing a gun in his hand as he slipped away into the early morning shadows, and yet, she said nothing about this at the trial. At the time, she thought she did the right thing considering the man she saw was a trusted authority in Jerome. She figured it would have been her word against his anyway.

The Queen knew the Villalpando family would be heartbroken when she kidnapped their baby boy. She also knew she could never have a child of her own and really believed she could give Enrique a better life. She was proud of the way she had raised Henry. He was now eighteen years old. He had grown into a fine young man and was now attending college. Henry looked a lot like his father, Francisco, and if Henry's parents could see him now, they too would be proud of him. In the back of her mind there was still a little guilt concerning Francisco's death that night at the dance. After all, she was the one who hired him as a bouncer. The guilt didn't last long though. She quickly dismissed the thought, and remembered how Francisco was the aggressor in the gunfight.

The Queen had witnessed much death in her life. She remembered seeing dead bodies when she was just a little girl living with her mother and the undertaker in New Orleans. She recalled years ago when she barely escaped her own death. It was a secret that she never revealed to anyone. When she was just a young teenager, a man had put a knife to her throat and raped her repeatedly. He said he would come back and kill her if she ever told anyone. Before the man left, he snuffed out his cigar on her breast leaving a painful burn, and later, a horrible scar.

She also remembered all the senseless deaths of the sporting ladies in Storyville. But the death that haunted her most was one she had arranged herself. She once hired a voodoo doctor to perform a cleansing on her. *Cleansing* was that brutal method used to intentionally abort unwanted babies of nameless *Johns*. She rationalized the decision by simply calling it a sacrifice that had to be made to remain employed as a sporting lady. After the ordeal, the voodoo doctor wrapped up the fully formed infant inside a newspaper and whisked him away, but not before she got a glimpse of the baby boy. That image, along with the constant regret, had haunted her for years.

Dozens of things were swirling through her mind. Nearly aloud, she asked, *"Why did Jelly Roll have to die this way? Why couldn't things have been different? Maybe it would have been better if Jelly Roll would have died in a car crash at the height of his career as he sped away in his brand new Cadillac being chased by his fanfare. Or getting shot in the back during a card game with thousands of dollars on the table would have been better than this. To die penniless and have his funeral in the poorest of black churches would have been the last thing Jelly would have wanted."*

She knew if Jelly Roll could have orchestrated his own demise, he would have gone out in style. He would have been carried down the streets of New Orleans in a long black hearse. There would have been a mile long parade, a brass band, and everyone would have been crying as they marched slowly to the graveyard. As it was, though, she was the only one crying. She buried her face in the petals of her fresh cut bouquet of roses, but they almost smelled phony......phony like the way she had lived her entire life, always pretending she was someone she wasn't.

She wished at this moment that the yellow roses would turn black. Then she could toss them into his grave, say farewell and be finished with all of it. She thought perhaps she would jump in the grave and go down with Jelly Roll. Suddenly her racing thoughts stopped cold when she remembered where Jelly Roll's ransomed soul might be going. The Queen, with her voodoo superstition, believed in her heart that when the clock struck midnight, the dark side would come for Jelly's soul. The Queen reached deep into her own tortured soul, made the sign of the cross and promised the man who had died in her arms she would hang on to him as long as she could. She would do everything in her power to prevent the mysterious forces from taking his ransomed soul back to the old French cemetery in New Orleans where the tomb of Marie Laveau and other voodoo priestesses would be waiting.

The other jazz-men who had served their time here on earth were also waiting for Jelly Roll Morton to reclaim his rightful position as their bandleader. Joe Oliver, Freddie Keppard, Budd Bolden, Tony Jackson, Jonny Dodds,

Bessie Smith and other departed jazz enthusiasts were waiting for Jelly Roll to accompany them and put the boys in the jazz band back together. The Queen now had a death grip on Jelly Roll's soul. His soul would now be suspended in purgatory. The jazz band and the boys on the other side would have to wait a while longer for their celestial reunion.

The Queen stood at Jelly Roll's grave frozen in time. How long had she been there? She couldn't recall, but when she looked up, she saw two gravediggers with their shovels in hand waiting respectfully on the fresh pile of dirt that would soon fill in Jelly Roll's grave. She was startled because she had not even heard the men walk up. She tossed her bouquet into his grave, said another prayer and walked back to Jelly Roll's Lincoln. Her husband Jack had been waiting there in the car for almost an hour and had become quite impatient and a little irritated with her.

Jack and The Queen drove Jelly Roll's Lincoln Sedan and all of his belongings back to Canyonville, Oregon. A few days later, they took a trip to Montpelier, Idaho, to get Jelly's 1938 Cadillac out of storage. It had been eight months since the accident in the snowstorm, and the overdue storage bill, plus interest, was now $237.16. Jelly Roll was nearly penniless when he passed-on. In fact, he still owed $35.00 on a rented piano and $48.69 for his short stay in the hospital. It was unknown how much in previous loans Jelly Roll Morton still owed Jack and The Queen.

Just two weeks before Jelly Roll Morton's death, on June 28, 1941, The Queen, with the help of her attorney Hugh E. Macbeth, prepared Jelly's last will and testament. Immediately after his death, she promptly filed a creditor's claim against the Morton estate. This later became controversial, but ultimately held up in court. Jelly Roll, had bequeathed everything including all of his music royalties to The Queen. To one of his half sisters he left the royalties from Tempo-Music, which had absolutely no value at all. To the other, he left one dollar.

Jelly was an intelligent, literate man and yet noticeably, the music company's name and even his own sister's names were misspelled on the document. Suspiciously, his own wife, Mable Morton, who was living back in New York, was not even mentioned in his will. The Queen's attorney had numerous legal gears turning to make sure that all of Ferdinand Joseph (Jelly Roll) Morton's estate and royalties immediately became due and payable to Anita Gonzales, aka Anita Ford. It wasn't long before Jelly Roll's royalty checks started rolling in.

Jack and The Queen eventually became tired of Oregon's cold damp weather and decided to move south to sunny California. They turned the operation of the Ford Café, over to their son Henry Ford in 1948. By this time, Henry had learned all the ropes of the restaurant business and was ready to make a go of it on his own. Henry and his wife ran the business for the next few years.

Last Will and Testament

In the Name of God, Amen, I, Ferdinand Joseph Morton residing at 1008 E 32 nd St.

of Los Angeles State of California

of the age of fifty one years, and being of sound and disposing mind and memory and not acting under duress, menace, fraud, or undue influence of any person whatever, do make, publish and declare this my last WILL AND TESTAMENT in the manner following, that is to say:

First: I give and bequeath to my sister, Amide Colas all my share of The Royalties, and interest in the Temple Music Co, Washington D,C.

To my sister Frances Morton, now married, I give and bequeath the sum of One Dollar ($1.00)

Secondly: I hereby devise and bequeath all the rest and residue of my estate, whether real or personal property or mixed, to my beloved Anita Gonzales who has been my beloved comforter, companion and help-meet for many years, and whose tender care I sincerely appreciate. This shall include all Ascap royalties, and Southern Music Co, melrose music Company and all property of every kind personal and otherwise wherever located.

Lastly, I hereby nominate and appoint Hugh E. Macbeth

the executor of this my last Will and Testament to serve without bond. and hereby revoke all former Wills by me made.

In Witness Whereof, I have hereunto set my hand and seal this 28th day of June, in the year of our Lord nineteen hundred and forty one

Ferdinand Joseph Morton (SEAL)

The foregoing instrument, consisting of one page including this one was at the date hereof, by the said Ferdinand Joseph Morton signed, and sealed and published as, and declared to us to be his last Will and Testament, in the presence of us, who, at his request and in his presence, and in the presence of each other, have subscribed our names as witnesses thereto

Hugh E. Macbeth
Residing at 1558 W. 37th St. Los Angeles Calif
Stella Alberta Johnson
Residing at 2340 Harmon St.
Los Angeles Calif.

Chapter 16

Mable was a Show Girl

Mable started her dance career with a vaudeville troupe.
Mable is in the back row on the left.

The news of Jelly Roll Morton's death was a complete surprise to his wife Mable. By the time she was notified of his passing, it was too late to travel from New York to California to attend Jelly's funeral. Mable was completely unaware of the events surrounding his death and certainly didn't know she had been out-trumped by The Queen. Jelly Roll's passing left Mable broke, alone and abandoned in a New York apartment.

Mable Bertrand was born in New Orleans. She had a difficult childhood and was raised in a convent after both of her parents died. As an adult, Mable was a petite woman weighing scarcely one hundred pounds. It is believed that she also worked as a sporting lady in Storyville, New Orleans under the name of Mable Stein. The name Mable Stein was listed in the Storyville Blue Book in 1914. The Blue Book had her address as 1426 Iberville Street, which formerly was a well know brothel called *The Custom House*. Mable loved to dance and soon made it her profession.

She started her dance career with a vaudeville troupe called *The Billy Arnet Dixieland Show*. Later, she worked her way to both the national stage as well as abroad including performing for The Queen of England at Buckingham Palace and the Follies Berger's in Paris, France. In the early 1920s, she also performed as a burlesque dancer in the Apollo Theatre in Harlem, New York. The Apollo Theatre is the most famous performance venue associated with African American entertainers and burlesque. This form of theatrical entertainment featured period humor, usually consisting of comedic skits, chorus lines or striptease.

It is said that Mable performed with the famous Florence Mills in *Dixie to Broadway*. The Broadway show had a seventy-seven performance run at the Broadhurst Theater in New York from October, 1924, through January of 1925.

Mable also performed with Florence Mills in the production of *Black Birds* from 1926 to 1927.

Mable's professional journey brought her to Chicago for the first time in the summer of 1927 when she landed a six-week engagement at the Monogram Theatre. Later that same summer, Mable was working as a specialty dancer at the Plantation Club in Chicago. Jelly Roll Morton was in the crowd, sipping champagne and watching the show when a pretty little octoroon showgirl named *Mable* caught his eye. After the show, Jelly Roll made his way backstage and waited for her. Their encounter was brief.

Mable said, *"After the performance, I didn't want to talk to anyone. All I wanted to do was to go to the hotel, get out of my costume, sponge off with alcohol and cool down. Chicago is hot and humid in the summer and the stage lights make it even hotter. I had asked the desk clerk to hold any calls for me, but Jelly Roll Morton found out where the dancers were staying and by bribing the bellman, got my name and room number. Jelly Roll telephoned the room, and I agreed to meet him in the lobby. We talked and hit it off immediately."*

Mable, or "May" as Jelly called her, was an exotic looking woman. Her father was a French Creole man and her mother was a Shawnee Indian. Jelly Roll eventually convinced May to leave her career behind and travel with him and his new jazz band, *The Red Hot Peppers*.

The Red Hot Peppers c.1926

Mable Bertrand and Ferdinand Morton were married in Gary, Indiana in November of 1927, and for the next twelve years, they traveled the country together. Mable had married Jelly Roll right at the height of his notoriety.

Both Jelly Roll and Mabel were known to be quite the hustlers. Mabel had a very timid personality and sat obediently by the bandstand as Jelly Roll played. As time went on, Mabel proved to be someone Jelly Roll could easily control. It was said that while Jelly Roll was performing, Mable would sometimes *work* the dance floor as a pickpocket, stealthily lifting jewelry and money from the pockets and purses of unsuspecting customers.

In 1935, Mabel stayed in New York and Jelly Roll went to Washington, D.C. allegedly to work on the side as a fight promoter. Mabel eventually followed him there, and it was in D.C. where Jelly Roll got into a nightclub brawl and was nearly stabbed to death. As soon as Jelly's wounds healed, they both moved back to New York.

In 1939 Jelly Roll Morton suffered a heart attack. His wife, Mable, took him to a New York hospital where he eventually recovered. After that episode, however, Jelly was never the same. After the attack, it became a chore just to climb the stairs to his New York apartment. Not only was Jelly Roll now in poor health, but his efforts to collect on his music royalties had been unproductive and the stress of it all was taking its toll. While Mabel did everything in her power for him, she could only watch as her husband, Jelly Roll Morton became a sick, broken down, bitter man.

When Jelly Roll took his final trip out west in 1940, he lied to May, telling her he was going to Los Angeles to visit his sick godmother Echo. Jelly said that she was no longer able to care for his godfather, Ed Hunter who was now blind. The truth was, his godmother, Echo had been dead for more than 3 months. A few days later Jelly wrote May a letter explaining that his godmother Echo had died before he got there. He explained how everything was gone;

including her diamonds and his poor godfather had been left with nothing but the shirt on his back.

Jelly Roll sent his wife Mable roughly ten letters and a very modest amount of money in the nine months he was attempting to make his return to fame. He started each letter with, "My Dearest Wife May." Jelly Roll sent this letter on January 17, 1941:

My Dearest Wife May,

Sorry I haven't written you more often. I did not want to write until I had some money to send you. Enclosed you will find $17.00. See if you can pay interest on the things that are most overdue. I feel sure we will be able to go to Mardi Grass in March. It will be warmer then. Maybe you could take a train there and I could meet you in New Orleans. I know how much that would mean to you. It's been hard getting a band together cause none of these cats want to work when they've not been paid. I'm feeling a little better, still having chest pains and sometimes find it hard to breathe.

Please May, don't worry. I'm sure things will turn out all right. Love, Ferd

Of course, the trip to New Orleans never came to pass. Jelly Roll's letters became even scarcer as his physical condition continued to deteriorate. It had been less than nine months since Jelly Roll left his wife May in their New York apartment. He was now lying on his deathbed in the L.A. County Hospital, in a room not much bigger than a broom closet. Jelly Roll's heart was losing the battle and he was now fading in and out of consciousness.

On June 28, 1941, the crafty Queen put a piece of paper in front of Jelly Roll to sign. It was his Last Will and Testament. The document seems to reveal that in his weakened condition, he couldn't even sign his own name, *Ferdinand Joseph Morton* on a straight line. The document written in The Queen's own handwriting began; *"I hereby bequeath to my beloved Anita Gonzales, who has been my beloved comforter, companion and helpmate for many years, and whose tender care I sincerely appreciate...."* The will stated that The Queen was to be the sole recipient of Jelly Roll Morton's estate, which included the millions in royalties that would one day be paid. It was signed by The Queen's lawyer, Hugh E. Macbeth and witnessed by her sister-in-law, Stella Johnson.

Did Jelly Roll really know what he was signing? Had Jelly become so delusional that he would sign anything that The Queen put in front of him? It certainly seems doubtful that Jelly Roll would completely exclude May, his own loving wife from his will. Being Jelly's Roll Morton's widow, Mable was, if nothing else, legally entitled to his estate. All she needed to do was to prove that they were married. Jelly had always kept their marriage license with him, safe in his wallet, but after his death the license never materialized.

Mabel Morton said, *"I remember the day Jelly and I got married very well. That morning we drove to Gary, Indiana, in Jelly Roll's car. We were married by the justice of the peace on November 10,*

1927 in the courthouse. We both signed our marriage license, and it was witnessed by the clerk. I always wanted to frame our marriage license and hang it on the wall, but Jelly Roll insisted on carrying it with him when he traveled. Some states had strict laws requiring entertainers to be married, and our marrage license was proof. After we were married, Jelly insisted that I give up my dancing in the theatrical business. He wanted me to travel with him and his 'Red Hot Peppers', band. When we traveled, we would always stay in the best hotels, we ate the best food, we drove the best cars, and we had the best clothes. Jelly knew all my sizes, and he would do most of the shopping. He would always buy me the most expensive clothes.... Price didn't matter to him. Jelly always told me, 'Never mind what it costs. We have the money today, never mind tomorrow.... Tomorrow will take care of itself'. I never learned to drive a car either. Jelly said I didn't need to learn and that he would take me anywhere I needed to go. He took care of everything." She added, "Some people say Jelly was hard to get along with, but I knew it was because he was a perfectionist. He was harder on himself than anybody else. I never had trouble with Jelly and other women. Often he would come home very late, but he always told me he was just working at a club, and I had no reason to worry."

For more than 12 years, Mabel Morton was Jelly Roll's true companion and comforter. She was there with Jelly Roll through sickness and in health. She was there for him through his accomplishments and through his struggles. She consoled him when he was down and was willing to do whatever it took to help keep him happy and healthy.

In many ways, Mabel deserved credit for much of Jelly Roll Morton's success. Her devotion to him was beyond measure. She cooked his meals, kept his suits cleaned and pressed and helped him pack when he traveled to his performances.

The news of Jelly Roll's death hit Mable like a bombshell. The minute she heard the terrible news, she sent a telegram to the funeral home explaining she could not possibly get there in time to attend her beloved husband's funeral. She wanted to know who was taking care of all the arrangements, but the information she received was sketchy. The Queen had been screening all phone calls and telegrams. On the registry under *Friends Who Sent Calls and Wires*, The Queen entered Mable's first name only and oddly left out her last name, Morton.

Only a few people were invited to Jelly Roll's funeral. A church that could have seated hundreds was virtually empty and the newspapers only casually mentioned his passing in the weekly obituaries. The man who claimed to have invented jazz simply faded away.

The four people below who sent telegrams were all notified too late to attend Jelly Roll's memorial service.

Mrs. Amide Colas, LA..Jelly Roll's half sister

Mrs. Mime Oliver, TX. ....Jelly Roll's half sister

Mrs. Mable, NY ....Jelly's wife, Mable Morton

Mr. R. J. Carew, W. D. C. ....Jelly's best friend

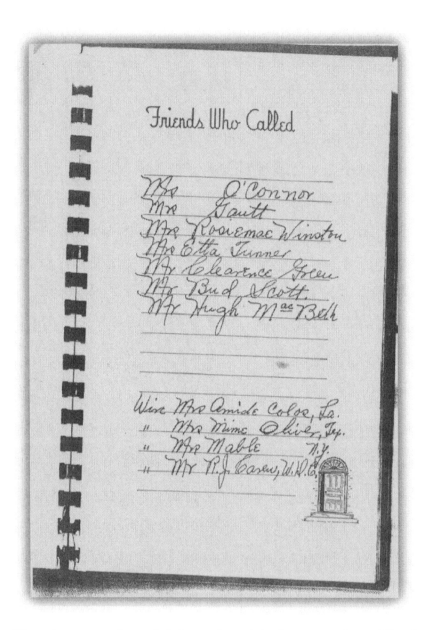

The above page is copied from the original guest register. The first seven entries are friends who phoned and the last entries are friends who sent telegrams. Notice the second to the last entry. It simply says Mrs. Mable, New York

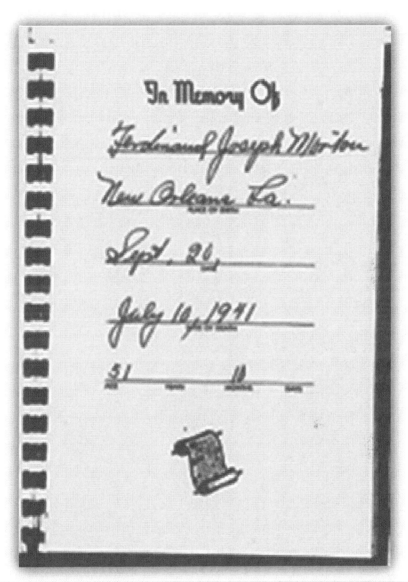

Chicago Daily Tribune

July 11, 1941. Ferdinand Morton 51 years, song composer, died yesterday In Los Angeles, Cal. He was the author of *Jelly Roll Blues*, *Mama Nita* the *Wolverine Blues*, and others.

In Mabel's resolve she said, *"I've been loved by a great man. I've watched Jelly dazzle the crowds with his music. I've watched a genius at work in the cold and lonely hours of the morning as he wrote on paper the music that played in his head. He was the first Jazz Band. All the others, like Ellington and Calloway and Basie and those, came after Jelly. He was so well liked by the white people, that he never had to play a colored engagement. Most of the colored places couldn't afford him anyway. The only time colored people saw him was when he dropped into a cabaret for a drink. I will always love my Jelly Roll. I did all I could for him. What else could I have done? I'll be so lost without him."*

Mabel Morton lived out the rest of her life in New York. She died in public housing in 1962 of natural causes.

About a month after Jelly Roll Morton's passing, this obituary was printed in the Los Angeles Times.

Jelly Roll Morton aka Ferdinand
Joseph La Mothe
Born: 20-Oct-1890
Birthplace: New Orleans, LA
Died: 10-Jul-1941
Location of death: Los Angeles, CA
Cause of death: Heart Failure
Remains Buried: Calvary
Cemetery, Los Angeles
Gender: Male
Race or Ethnicity: Black
Occupation: Jazz Musician,
Pianist
Father: Edward LeMothe
Mother: Louise Monette
Girlfriends: Anita Gonzales &
Mable Bertrand

Ferdinand Joseph La Mothe, better known as Jelly Roll Morton, was the pioneer of modern American Jazz. He grew up in New Orleans and began playing in brothels and saloons when he was still a boy. In the 1920's he performed solo a series of recordings he made in Chicago for RCA Victor. He is particularly remembered for his band, the "Red Hot Peppers." Morton is often credited with mixing individual improvisation with rehearsed group arrangements, a form that became the staple of Jazz. His best-known tunes included Jelly Roll Blues, King Porter Stomp and the Black Bottom Stomp. His diamond studded front tooth sparkled in the stage lights when he performed and is almost a legend in itself. Many mourn his passing. Jelly Roll Morton, probably did more than any other one man to perpetuate one of America's most valuable native musical forms. The Blues from which stemmed such developments as Jazz, modern swing and the boogie woogie. He passed away at the age of 50.

Chapter 17

Royalties Start Rolling In

Jack and Anita Ford's Topanga Beach Auto Court California

It wasn't long before Jelly Roll Morton's music royalties started rolling in. With the help of this extra money, Jack and The Queen moved to sunny California and bought another business. It was an upscale motel on seven acres located at the bottom of Topanga Canyon near Malibu Beach. It was called the Topanga Beach Auto Court.

The Fords were now living in style thanks to Jelly Roll's royalties. Ironically, Jelly Roll Morton's grave sat unmarked and overgrown with weeds. His gravesite had remained without a headstone for more than ten years. It seemed the world had completely forgotten about the musical genius who rested below.

The *Southern California Hot Jazz Society* members were appalled by the lack of consideration shown for one of their cherished musicians. Jelly Roll Morton had been a dominant figure in the birth and development of jazz and they emphatically expressed that he deserved more respect than just a hole in the ground. The society decided to hold a benefit concert to raise funds for a plaque and permanent care for his gravesite. Their concert was less than a week away and the lineup of entertainers for the event was impressive. They were expecting a full house and most of the tickets were sold. The memorial concert almost came to a screeching halt when out of the blue, a woman named Anita Ford (The Queen) called and angrily insisted the project be stopped. She simply would not allow the jazz society to purchase a headstone for Jelly Roll Morton's grave. She emphatically informed them that she would not allow a charitable undertaking that might embarrass the memory of her dearly departed husband, Jelly Roll Morton. She invited the members to visit her at the Topanga Beach Auto Court to discuss the situation. Honoring The Queen's invitation, a few society members went to Malibu the following day. Despite her rather condescending attitude on the phone the previous day, she actually seemed pleased to see the members once they arrived. She greeted them at the door with a friendly smile and introduced herself and her husband as Mr. and Mrs. J. F. Ford.

A conversation according to the jazz society

"Mrs. Ford was a gracious host and invited us in. She was a pretty woman wearing heavy makeup and a lot of diamond jewelry. She spoke warmly with a pronounced New Orleans accent." The jazz society member explained, "We sat comfortably on the plush red velvet sofa in the living room. The room was filled with art and expensive furnishings. It looked remarkably like a parlor in a bordello. Hanging on the wall in the living room was a large theatrical blowup of a beautiful, nearly nude girl. Noticing our interest in the picture, Mrs. Ford said, *"That's my granddaughter, Aleene. She looks a lot like I did in my younger days. She's a striptease dancer at the Follies Theater. By the way, I'm fixing a batch of fried chicken. Would you please stay and have some?"* The jazz members accepted her offer. Rising from her chair, she walked toward the kitchen and added, *"I'm famous for my fried chicken and peach pie you know."* A few moments later, she returned with a plate of hot crispy fried chicken and an ice-cold beer for each of them. They ate and listened as she spoke.

"Jelly Roll came to visit me and my little brother, Dink Johnson, at my Arcade Saloon in Las Vegas before the First World War. He sure looked sharp in those days, always dressing in the latest style. We put our money together and Jelly and I bought a hotel here in California years ago...in 1918...I think. It was the hotel that Jelly Roll named after me, The Anita Hotel. He played in the club next door. My job was to manage the rooms, but he wouldn't let me do any work at the hotel so we ended up selling it. We split up for a brief time, so I moved to Jerome, Arizona, for a few months and managed the City Café and a few of the upstairs rooms. Ferddy followed me there but he didn't stay. He just didn't like the heat. Shortly after that, we got back together, and we moved to San Francisco where we ran The Jupiter Club. I spent a lot of money fixing up the place. My little brother, Dink, was still managing The Arcade for me in Las Vegas, that's where most of my money came from." (Often in her conversation, she would substitute Ferddy for Jelly Roll.) *"Jelly Roll refused to let me work. He was very old-fashioned that way. It was his pride and his jealousy I guess. He always wanted to be the one to take care of me. Then Ferddy started gambling and got in a fight with the police, so we had to close down "The Jupiter."*

She paused for a moment as she reflected back to that time. Regaining her thoughts, she smiled and continued. *"Did you know Ferddy and I were sweethearts years ago back in New Orleans? We actually grew up knowing each other's families. My brothers, Bill and Dink played music with Ferddy and Freddy Keppard in the Creole Band at the Orpheum Theater. I had a good voice in those days and loved to sing the old blues songs, but never with Jelly. I begged to sing in his band but he would never let me. I did, however, sing some with my brother, Dink. Dink still plays the piano. He actually lives in Santa Barbara now. He owns a restaurant and in the evenings he plays piano there. It's called Dink's Place. My older brother, Bill, has a business in Texas and I hear he still plays some too. Bill is a fantastic bass player...but I seldom see either of them. "*

The Queen, realizing the jazz society was there to hear about Jelly Roll, continued her dialogue. *"Ferddy and I were married in 1919 and we traveled a lot back in those days. We went up the west coast to Oregon and Washington for several months...even into Canada and Alaska. Everywhere we went, people loved his music. Did you know he wrote a couple of tunes for me? They were called Sweet Anita-Mine and Mama-Nita. I wrote the lyrics to Dead Man Blues. Jelly Roll put it to music and recorded it here in Los Angeles long ago, but I don't know if it ever came out. He did a lot of recordings after we broke up. He left and went back East. He moved around a lot and finally settled in New York. I guess I've moved some, too. I was born in Alabama. I've lived in New Orleans, Los Angeles, Las Vegas, and let me see."* She counted on her fingers as she recalled the places she lived in order, *"San Francisco, New York, Washington, Arizona and Oregon.... I've also been to Canada, Alaska and Old Mexico. Jelly used to play piano in a bar in Tijuana, Mexico called 'The Kansas City Bar'. Funny, name for a bar in Mexico huh? A lot of people from California would go to Old Mexico to drink and hear the music during the U.S. prohibition. That's about the time Ferddy and I split up and went our separate ways. I think he lived with some woman for a while in New York."*

Looking a little nervous, she lit another cigarette. She never even noticed she still had one burning in the ashtray. She took a couple of deep drags. Regaining her thoughts she said, *"I sold the Arcade in Las Vegas and moved back to Jerome, Arizona in the early, '20s. I ran a couple of businesses there for the next eight or nine years. Jerome was a wild place...a copper mining town on the side of a mountain. That's where I met Jack Ford. Later on, the two of us moved to Oregon. That was in the early '30s. We ran our Ford Café and Gas Station there in Canyonville and did quite well considering it was during the depression. We lived there a little over twenty years. And now we're back here in Malibu, California, running this motor court."*

The jazz society members were fascinated with her story and encouraged her to talk. *"Jelly Roll and I always kept in touch with each other, you know. He would always send me his latest records. Sometimes they would arrive broken. I used to have a lot more of Jelly's records, but a lot of them got lost or broken over the years."* She then pointed to a bookcase near the door. A handsome mahogany phonograph player stood proudly in the corner and a stack of records sat on the nearby bookcase. The jazz members were sure that the stack included some of Morton's rare old 78-rpm records.

Wiping tears from her eyes, she concluded, *"Jelly Roll was a musical genius, I do miss him. He died in my arms you know. Jelly told me I was the only woman he ever truly loved."* She ended the conversation with, *"I'll call tomorrow and order his headstone."*

She bought the headstone as promised and had these words inscribed. REST IN PEACE FERDINAND MORTON, JELLY ROLL   1890–1941

Photo of the headstone

In 1950, The Queen agreed to be interviewed by Bob Kirstein on the weekly radio show called Doctor Jazz, broadcasting on KFMV FM-94.7. The Station was located on Sunset Boulevard in Hollywood, California. The Queen began the interview on the radio station by saying, *"Hello, everybody. It's indeed a great pleasure to be here tonight in the studio, and hear some of the old jazz pieces of, er, Jelly Roll's. I'm very delighted- all elated. Thank you."*

The program was interspersed with Jelly Roll's records and lasted about a half hour. All through the interview, The Queen claimed to have been Jelly Roll's Morton's widow, Anita Gonzales Morton. Of course, she wasn't. At the time of Jelly's death, and for the last thirty years, she had been married to Jack Ford.

Kid Ory, one of the boys of the Red Hot Pepper band was also at the interview. At one of the breaks, Kid Ory pulled the manager aside and informed him that The Queen was not Jelly Roll's wife. He said, *"I know Jelly's wife very well. Her name is Mable Morton, and she often traveled with us and the Red Hot Peppers band. I've eaten gumbo at their house in New York many times, but I've never seen this woman before. Who is she?"*

After that, things started to heat up and uncomfortable questions were being asked. The Queen, fearing her cover would be exposed, abruptly ended the interview and sped away in Jelly Roll's long black 1938 Cadillac. They never saw her again.

On April 24, 1952, a little over a year after the jazz society's visit, The Queen met her maker. She died of the same complications as Jelly Roll Morton and was buried in the Calvary Cemetery in Los Angeles, just a short walk from Jelly Roll's grave.

Just before she died, The Queen made Jack Ford promise to file falsified statements on her death certificate. She surely didn't want her son Henry to know she was not his real mother, nor did she want him to know she was African American. The deceit on her death certificate was surely a plan to protect young Henry Ford and his family. Jack, being the *informant* on her death certificate, affirmed she was born in old Mexico. Jack also stated her father was a Mexican man named Enrique V. Gonzales.

The Queen also instructed Jack Ford never to let Henry know about the Johnson side of her family. Jack now had to arrange two funerals. One was for the Ford family where she was still claiming to be Mexican and the mother of Henry Ford, *(Enrique Villalpando)*. The second funeral was held a few days later for the Johnsons, her biological family. The Queen also lied about her age. She was actually seventy, not sixty as recorded at the time of her death. Jack documented her birth date to be April 13, 1892. Her true birth date, however, was April 13, 1883, nine years earlier.

The Queen was born Bessie Julia Johnson in Montgomery, Alabama. Her mother's name was Hattie Johnson, and she was not Mexican. The Queen was, what was then called a mulatto, a product of both black and white parents. All the years The Queen spent bleaching her skin had caused her complexion to become gray and ashy, and her dark pigment to separate into spots. It must have been a wearisome task to live a double life, full of deception, denying her African heritage and lying about her age and family history.

After The Queen's death, Jack Ford took possession of all her personal effects including her diamond jewelry and her old steamer trunk filled with Jelly Roll Morton's personal property. Because of all the document fraud, The Queen's natural daughter, Hattie, and eventually even her two granddaughters, Aleene and Rosemary, inherited most of Jelly Roll Morton's music royalties.

Copy of Anita Julia Ford's death certificate

Timeline for The Queen

1.	**1883 Born April 13,** in Montgomery Alabama. Given name **Bessie Julia Johnson.**
2.	**1887 Bessie Johnson, Age 5,** moved to New Orleans with her mother and family. They lived with the undertaker where her three younger brothers were born.
3.	**1900 Bessie Julia Seymour, Age 17,** wife/common law wife of Fred Seymour. They had a daughter and named her Hattie.
4.	**1902–1908 Julia Johnson, Age 20,** worked as a first class sporting lady in Storyville, the red-light district of New Orleans and is listed in the blue book under that name.
5.	**1909–1917 Mamacita Juanita, Age 26,** was the madam of her own business, the Arcade Saloon in Las Vegas, Nevada's red-light district.
6.	**1918–1922 Anita Morton, Age 35,** aka Mama-Nita and Anita Gonzales, married to the famous Jazz composer Jelly Roll Morton.
7.	**1922–1928 The Cuban Queen, Age 39,** was known as Annie Johnson and/or The Cuban Queen. She operated The Cuban Queen Bordello and a billiard parlor in the copper mining town of Jerome, Arizona.
8.	**1928–1946 Mrs. Anita Ford, Age 45,** and her accomplice Jack Ford kidnapped a boy from Jerome, Az. and moved to Canyonville, Oregon where they ran the Ford Café and Gas Station.
9.	**1941 Anita Morton, Age 58,** for a brief time in 1941 claimed to be Jelly Roll Morton's wife even though she was married to Jack Ford. She was the person responsible for the contents of Jelly Roll's last will and testament, thereby inheriting all of Jelly Roll Morton's assets.
10.	**1947–1952 Mrs. J. F. Ford, Age 64,** moved to California. She and Jack Ford bought the Topanga Beach Auto Court near Malibu Beach.
11.	**1952 Anita Julia Ford, Age 69,** died April 21, 1952 and was buried in the Calvary Cemetery in Los Angeles, CA. just a short walk from Jelly Roll Morton's grave.

Chapter 18

Grandpa Jack and the
Big Black Cadillac

Ford's Cafe and Gas Station, Canyonville, Oregon c. 1948

Henry is in the chef's hat holding his son Mike. The woman to his left is Anita Ford (The Queen). Notice Jelly Roll Morton's 1938 Cadillac is parked in the background.

For years after mid-1941, Jelly Roll's long, sleek, black Cadillac was parked at the rear of the Ford's restaurant. Jack Ford always maintained it in immaculate condition.

Jack Ford, *now called Grandpa Jack,* would often babysit Henry's son Mike. Mike wasn't old enough to go to school yet, so sometimes Grandpa Jack would keep his grandson while he did chores and fed the animals.

⇐ *Grandpa Jack and Mike Ford*

As the story goes, when little Mike was naughty, his Grandpa Jack would take him out in back of the Ford Café and put the young boy in Jelly Roll's big black 1938 Cadillac. Jack would slam the door and Mike would have to sit in the car in *"time-out"* until he promised to be good. Mike said, *"I remember that. I hated sitting in that car more than anything. It was cold in there, very creepy, and it smelled weird. All my Grandpa Jack would have to do was ask me in that big scary voice, 'Do you want to have to sit in Jelly's big black Cadillac?' I would start crying and begged him. 'Please don't put me in the big black car, I promise I'll be good.'"*

At the time, little Mike had no idea why his Grandpa Jack called the car *Jelly's big black Cadillac.* Apparently, when Jelly Roll was living in New York, he was so broke he couldn't even afford to put gas in the car. For extra income, Jelly Roll would rent out his 1938 Cadillac to a funeral home. Perhaps there were a few lingering spirits in the car, and that's why little Mike hated it so.

Approximately three months after The Queen's death, Jack Ford was sitting alone in a bar in Santa Monica, California. All the patrons were drinking beer and watching a boxing match on television. The fight was between a black prizefighter and a white prizefighter. Some say it was Jack's Irish blood, but he always seemed to get loud and obnoxious when he had a few too many. He was shouting, *"Kill that son-of-a-bitch...Kill that Nigger...Kill him!"*

Two young men also watching the fight were getting tired of Jack's loud mouth and racial slurs, so they confronted him. In his own defense Jack said, *"Hey, I have nothing against Negros. I've worked with them all my life. Hell, I even married one! Ever hear of Jelly Roll Morton? Well, we were married to the same black woman...and I can prove it!"*

The two young men were fresh out of college. They had studied the jazz movement in school and were familiar with Jelly Roll Morton's fame. Jack invited the two men to follow him out to the parking lot where he showed them Jelly Roll Morton's vintage 1938 Cadillac. The Caddy was black, sleek and shiny. Being a first-rate mechanic, Jack kept the car well tuned and the big engine purred like a kitten. The young men seemed impressed with the car, but a little skeptical as to its previous owner being Jelly Roll Morton. Not to be deterred by their skepticism, Jack insisted the two men follow him home. Leaning against the car for balance, Jack boasted, *"Come on, I'll show you more!"*

They followed Jack down the Pacific Coast Highway to Malibu and then to his Topanga Beach Auto Court. Once inside, Jack served up another round of beers. He left the room momentarily and returned with The Queen's scrapbook and a large collection of Jelly Roll Morton's memorabilia. According to Jack Ford, in the early 1940s, Jelly Roll Morton was flat broke and begged his ex-wife Anita for money. Jack boasted that he had given Jelly Roll Morton a loan so he could put a new band together, do some promoting, and try to get his music career back on track. Then, Jelly Roll died still owing him the money. Jack told them how back in 1919, Jelly's wife, Anita, bought Jelly Roll a thirty point diamond as a wedding present and how Jelly had the diamond mounted in gold and set into his front tooth. Saturated with liquid courage, Jack then admitted something he had never told anyone before. With a noticeable slur in his speech, he began;

"Want to hear a true story about Jelly Roll? It was the night before Jelly Roll's funeral. I went down to the morgue, picked the lock and slipped into the funeral parlor through a side door in the middle of the night. I was good at picking locks. There were several coffins with dead folks in there, but I knew which one was Jelly's, because Anita and I were there early that morning making his final funeral arrangements. With my flashlight, I found Jelly's coffin and opened the lid. I shined my light on that coon's cold dead body, and I could see the sparkle of that diamond still in his tooth. I took out my pocketknife and started digging. Believe me, I'm no dentist...and it sure left a nasty hole."

Noticing the disturbed look on the two young men's faces Jack added, *"Hey, to my way of thinking it was only fair that I was the one to get it. That cat died still owning me a bunch of money! That diamond my wife gave him was worth more than a thousand dollars back then...probably three times that now. I wasn't gonna let that swindler Jelly take it to his grave."*

It was apparent to the men that Jack didn't care much for Jelly Roll. It was quite obvious how jealous Jack was of his wife's past relationship with him. Jack then explained how he tried to close Jelly's cold lips so no one would notice the diamond was missing. He explained how Jelly's lips seemed to be frozen apart so he gave up, closed the lid to the coffin and headed for the door. Jack was certain he was the only one at the morgue that night, but recalled how he just about jumped out of his skin when he thought he heard the Baby Grand Piano in the funeral parlor start playing one of Jelly Roll's tunes called *Dead Man Blues*. He still seemed a bit haunted by the memories of that night.

Then, gaining his composure and feeling vindicated, Jack smiled broadly, pointed to his tooth and announced, *"This is Jelly Roll Morton's famous diamond!"* Seeing the diamond right there in Jack's tooth definitely made believers of the young men. If the story he told is true, then Jack Ford was the thief who took the diamond from Jelly Roll Morton's cold dead body the night before the funeral. Did Jack steal the diamond under The Queen's directions or did he commit this crime on his own? It seems no one will ever know the answer to this question.

In 1958, six years after The Queen's death, Jack Ford received a lump sum of over twelve thousand dollars in a royalty check from Jelly Roll Morton's estate. With that money, Jack took a trip to Ireland to visit some of his relatives. Upon returning to California, Jack suddenly, and without warning, had a heart attack at the airport and died on the way to the hospital. After hearing of Jack's death, Henry immediately made the trip to California. By this time, he was running his own successful restaurant and a piano bar called Henry Ford's at 9589 Barbur Boulevard in Portland, Oregon.

When he arrived in Malibu, The Queen's entire diamond collection was again missing. Even the famed thirty point diamond was no longer in Jack's tooth. Henry had no idea as to where they could have gone. The diamonds were surely worth a considerable sum, but there was really no way to verify they even existed.

Henry then began the task of settling his parents' estate. As he searched through their property, he found an old steamer trunk belonging to his mother. Included in the trunk was a scrapbook containing a collection of Jelly Roll Morton's memorabilia. Henry didn't pay much attention to the trunk and for the next forty years, it sat in the spare bedroom collecting dust.

Sometime around 1995, Mike Ford received a phone call while working at the Henry Ford restaurant in Portland, Oregon. The woman on the other end of the phone asked to speak to Henry Ford. Mike said, *"Certainly, may I tell him who is calling?"* The woman on the other end of the phone said, *"My name is Angelina. I'm his big sister."* Mike thought that was a strange statement because he believed his dad was an only child. Mike gave the phone to his dad Henry, who was almost seventy years old at that time. About a minute into the phone conversation, Henry went into the office to speak in private. He spoke on the phone to the stranger for about fifteen minutes.

Mike said, *"When dad came out of the office, he looked a little bewildered, so I asked who the strange caller was? He replied, 'It was just a wrong number' and that was all he ever said about the phone call."*

The caller was Angelina Parra, the same person who had written the letters to the Jerome archives so many years ago looking for her little brother Enrique Villalpando. Angeline had finally found her little brother who had been kidnapped back in 1927. She later sent Henry a package containing his baptismal record along with articles from an Arizona newspaper on the death and trial of a Francisco Villalpando in 1924. Another article pertained to the 1927 death of a woman named Guadalupe Villalpando. Both were from Jerome, Arizona.

It took Henry a while, but the picture soon became clear how he was kidnapped from his biological family and taken to Canyonville, Oregon. His name was not Henry Ford, but Enrique Villalpando. At seventy years old, he couldn't believe his whole life had been based on deceit. The Queen had covered her tracks well. The Villalpando family had also remained clueless for seventy years as to what happened to their brother Enrique, that hot August night in Jerome, Arizona.

Henry told only his wife what he had learned. Regrettably, Henry Ford died one year later without ever meeting his biological Villalpando family. After Henry's death in 1996, his wife prepared his memorial service and only then did she tell the family about their discovery. All of Jelly Roll's memorabilia contained in the old steamer trunk was turned over to the proper authorities and is now displayed in the Louisiana State Museum Jazz Collection.

Jelly Roll Morton was inducted into the Big Band and Jazz Hall of Fame in 1982 and into the Rock and Roll Hall of Fame in 1998.

Chapter 19

Henry Ford

*Enrique Villalpando, aka
Henry Ford 1923–1996*

Henry Ford had taken over the operation of Ford's Café in Canyonville, Oregon in 1948, while Jack and Anita Ford moved to California and bought the upscale Topanga Beach Auto Court. After Jack Ford's death in 1956, the Ford Café continued to serve weary travelers generous plates of fried chicken, steaks, baked ham and pies.

The sign on the billboard read "YOU CAN PASS BY FORD'S BUT DON'T LET FORD'S PASS YOU BY."

A few years later, the government seized the Ford property by eminent domain. It was bulldozed to make way for the new California Interstate 5. Henry took the compensation and moved to Portland, Oregon. In 1955, Henry acquired the landmark, *Redmond's on the Hill Restaurant* on Barbur Boulevard in Southwest Portland. In 1961 a major remodel took place, and it soon became a first class restaurant and piano bar. He simply named it "HENRY FORD'S."

For over 40 years the huge sign lit up the Oregon sky.
Henry Ford's was at 9589 S.W. Barbur Boulevard, Portland, Oregon

On the back of the new Henry Ford's menu was a little history about how the business got started.

The menu read "Famous for great food since 1927." The menu goes on to tell how Jack and Anita Ford opened the small cafe and gas station on Highway 99 in Canyonville, Oregon.

Henry Fords' became more than just a cafe. It became a world-class fine dining service with quality cuisine, serving USDA prime beef selections, along with traditional steakhouse fare, seafood choices and fine wine offerings.

Portland Restaurant Listings and Reviews

Henry Ford's is a Portland establishment that has been around since the late '40s and luckily, hasn't changed much. In an age of pseudo-European yuppie dining, when people only act as if they enjoy the food, as they set in uncomfortably skinny seats. Henry Ford's is a real experience and a breath of retro and meaty air. It is architecturally attractive with flocked red wallpaper and comfortable seating. The restaurant's ambiance is mysterious and historic. The food is traditional fare, served with *real* class. There is a very popular bar with a view of a splendid foaming fountain, from which you MUST order a special drink, preferably a hard-liquor concoction. The food also happens to be delicious. The menu appetizers are a scrumptious delight. They include prawn cocktail, crab and escargot. Dinner, of course, is a meat lover's dream. Steak is recommended-Porterhouse or New York Strip- but the fresh fish and the savory 20-ounce lobster tail are also options. Dinner comes with biscuits, green salad and baked potato. And where else can you get a side dish of cooked yams glazed in brown sugar? TR *9589 S.W. Barbur Boulevard, 245-2434. Open daily for dinner. Moderate to Expensive*

"The Unique Guide to Portland's Fine Dinning"

Places like Henry Ford's are becoming few and far between, especially in a society where everything is the same. There are millions of Red Lobsters or Olive Gardens. Henry Ford's is unusual. This small dark bar in the back of a brightly lit restaurant looks as though it has been hermetically preserved since the days of the "Rat Pack." People flock to Henry Ford's including celebrities like Frank Sinatra, Dean Martin and Clark Gable. No other bar in Portland could bring under one roof, such a varied crowd. The Teens in prom dresses, middle-aged men in Harley Davidson leather jackets and devotees of the Columbia Sportswear, all come. At Henry Fords' the food is incredible, the service exceptional, the atmosphere is a little mysterious with a retro-décor. **PHONE AHEAD FOR RESERVATIONS: 245-2434**

"Portland Food, Restaurant & Bar Reviews"

Henry Ford's Restaurant and Piano Bar is a breath of fresh air. The elegant dining area is located downstairs near the garden patio. Enjoy a juicy steak, moist chicken or succulent seafood dishes and choose from an extensive wine list. There is the gorgeous windowed bar from which you see a flame throwing, foaming fountain. You can order a cocktail and watch the fountain while you wait to be seated in the architecturally beautiful dining room. There you'll find friendly, efficient, old-school waiters running the dining room. The seating is spacious and comfortable. Henry Ford's features live music on the weekends. **245-2434**

"Top Ten Night Spots"

Henry Ford's on Barbur Boulevard, Portland, Oregon, ranks among the **'Top Ten Steak-Houses'** in the USA. Smooooth is the sound from the keyboard. The interior of this landmark restaurant is covered in red velvet wallpaper and shadow art. Henry Ford's definitely has an aura of One-Eyed Jack with a dash of Black Lodge. Outside is an odd, but fascinating soap bubble and flame jet fountain that spews bubbles and flames ten feet high. The food, atmosphere and the music are excellent. **Call for Reservations 245-2434**

Certain conformities must be evident to the governing board to be honored on the prestigious "TOP TEN LIST."

Top 10 USD Steak-Houses Standards and Rules

A top 10 USDA Steakhouse is a fine dining establishment that sets the standards by which the finest steakhouse are defined. They epitomize dining excellence in all aspects of the culinary experience, quality of steakhouse, fine wine offerings, atmosphere ambiance consistent presentation, dining accommodations and world-class service.

1. Must demonstrate an exceptional history of providing great dining experiences from time of reservation to the diner's departure with a focus on decor, environment, and quality of cuisine, wine offerings and world class dining service.
2. Must feature USDA Prime Beef menu selections along with traditional steakhouse fare including fine seafood choices.
3. Exemplify the ambiance and decor of a white tablecloth environment.
4. Offer a minimum depth of one hundred wine labels representing popular wine regions in the US and the world.

Henry Ford's was well known throughout the Northwest. For decades, Henry Ford greeted his customers at the door in a dinner jacket. His waiters were dressed in tuxedos, and the food was exceptional. On the weekend nights, the line would stretch out the door and into the parking lot. Patrons would usually find standing room only at the piano bar.

Henry's customers included celebrities like Dean Martin, Sammy Davis Jr.,
Frank Sinatra, Clark Gable and many others.

Henry Ford's Piano Bar

Henry Ford shaking hands with customer c. 1994

Henry had a magical ability to draw an amazingly diverse crowd. He was always warm and welcoming and never met a stranger. He was always friendly and greeted people with a smile and a big strong handshake. He operated his restaurant and piano bar in Portland for forty-one years. Henry Ford passed away in March of 1996 at the age of seventy-two, leaving Henry Ford's Restaurant and Piano Bar to his family.

Oregonian newspaper obituary

Mass will be held at 11:00 a.m. Wednesday, March 6, 1996 in St. Mary's Cathedral for restaurant owner, Henry V. Ford, who died of cancer at the age of 72. Mr. Ford was born Aug 15, 1923 in Jerome Az. His parents Francisco and Guadalupe Villalpando died before his 4th birthday and he was adopted by a local miner and his wife, Jack and Anita Ford. He moved to Canyonville, Oregon, when he was four years old. Henry attended the University of Oregon. He acquired the landmark, Redmond's On the Hill Restaurant in Southwest Portland in 1955, renaming it Henry Ford's. He was involved in its operation for 41 years. Surviving are his wife Jeanne, son's Michael and Rick, daughter Patricia and five grand children. Interment will be in Mount Calvary Cemetery. The families suggest remembrances to the American Cancer Society.

Soon after Henry's passing, unexplainable things began to happen in the restaurant. At times, it seemed the whole building was vibrating and strange noises could be heard. Carl Metzler, a long time bartender at Henry Ford's recalled, *"Things just weren't the same after Henry passed. Strange things began to happen. The lights would flicker on and off, and cocktail glasses would slide off their shelves and shatter on the floor. One night, a portrait of Henry that had been bolted to the wall for thirty years, came crashing down.*

However, the most disturbing incident actually happened more than once. Each night, I would lean all the bar stools up against the bar so I could sweep and mop the floors. They always stayed that way until the next day. On several occasions, when I arrived to work the next day and unlocked the door, it was quite upsetting to see that a couple *of the bar stools were pushed away from the bar as if someone had been sitting there after we closed. As far as I knew, I had the only key to the place, and I <u>never</u> forgot to lock the door when I left."*

Carl also claimed that when he was cleaning up after hours, he would often see the dark ghostly figure of a well-dressed black woman rushing past the back bar mirrors. The woman always seemed to be very angry. Could it have been?

Another claim was from Dorothy Hackett, a sixty-five-year-old cocktail waitress who everyone called Dottie. Dottie was well-liked and served drinks at Henry Ford's restaurant and bar for several years. She claimed when the light was just right you could still see Henry's refection in the back bar mirror, straight across from where he sat on his favorite bar stool.

Dottie said, *"Honey,* (she called everyone Honey) *Henry's spirit still hangs around here watching over us. He has a favorite seat at the bar and customers who make the mistake of sitting on 'his stool' don't sit there long. They always feel a little odd, like they don't belong in that seat. They quickly move to another or just stand. That was Henry's seat. He sat on that stool for forty-one years drinking his Whiskey and Coke, and watching over his operation. Rest his soul, he was a real gem."*

Some might say The Queen should be credited with some of Henry Ford's success. The small boy, Enrique Villalpando, kidnapped from his home in Jerome, Arizona in 1927, became a larger than life, very successful restaurateur. The Queen left Henry with something money couldn't buy. She taught him her strong work ethics and gave him the unshakable confidence he needed to become the owner of one of the top ten steak houses in the USA. In turn, Henry Ford passed that ability on to his own family. They too became successful restaurant owners. Places like Henry Ford's are few and far between.

After Henry's death, his sons ran the Henry Ford restaurant for a few years. The building however, had seen better days and needed extensive renovation. In 2003, the restaurant and property was sold to a land developer. A huge dumpster soon sat next to the famous "flame-throwing bubbling fountain" while demolition began to make room for a row of townhouses. Henry Ford's piano bar was silenced, and the doors were closed and locked for the last time.

A special thanks to Mike Ford for all the family photos and valuable information.

Mike is the young boy standing with his dad Henry Ford, (Enrique Villalpando) grandson of Anita Ford aka "The Cuban Queen."

Chapter 20

A Black Rose for the Cuban Queen

I'll never forget the ghostly image I witnessed on that crisp November morning. From that day on, and for reasons I still haven't figured out, I had the most insatiable hunger to dig into this woman's life. As a result, I spent endless hours researching her entire mortal existence. It was as if she had me in her grip and for some reason was constantly tormenting me. Maybe she wanted her story to be documented before the old Cuban Queen building was demolished. Perhaps she wanted some sort of recognition or maybe even forgiveness.

As I followed all the twists and turns of a not-so-significant madam from the 1920s, I began to realize how it was affecting my own daily responsibilities. I knew I really needed to get on with my own life. I needed a solution to end all this nonsense.

Early one evening, I had this strange urge to go back to the Cuban Queen's bordello in Jerome. I took the short drive up the mountain and parked my car in front of the deserted bordello. I just sat there for a moment recalling the events of my last visit, which, by the way, still seemed a little disturbing. Gathering a little courage, I walked up to the doorstep. I just stood there and listened for a moment. All I could hear was the slight sound of the wind rustling through an old Paradise tree. I called out somewhat timidly, *"Hello"* and waited. There was no reply. Then, with a little more authority, but still softly I asked, *"Are you The Cuban Queen?"* I waited a moment more, but still nothing. I took in a deep breath and let it out with a sigh. I was almost feeling a little disappointed that there had been no response, and then I quickly realized how foolish this must look. Was I actually trying to talk to a ghost?

I remembered how shaken I was the last time I was here and I wondered why she decided to reveal herself to me that day. Perhaps she was restless and just playing with me. Was it possible her spirit could have been attached to that old queen-of-clubs playing card I picked up? Whatever the reason, she certainly got my attention.

I had always been a little skeptical when I would hear of someone seeing a ghost, but after that brief encounter, I seem to have become somewhat of a believer. That November morning, I definitely saw a spirit, a ghost, an apparition or whatever you want to call it, with my own eyes. Something, or someone, was undeniably there. The figure presented herself as a dark skinned woman adorned in diamonds. She gave me a little smile, just enough to reveal a slight sparkle that appeared to come from one of her front teeth. The figure faded gradually and then just seemed to float away.

Even though I have never been a believer in witchcraft or voodoo, I was reminded of the advice from Jelly Roll Morton's Godmother Echo, the self-proclaimed voodoo witch. Echo claimed that by giving someone a black rose, *"you would be forever liberated from whatever issues that have you bound."*

A month later, I returned to The Cuban Queen Bordello, but this time I was a little more prepared. I opened my jacket and pulled out a black silk rose that I had purchased the day before. I must admit, I did this with some degree of reluctance, and in fact, at times it almost seemed absurd.

As I stood there on the steps of the bordello, I kept telling myself, "Whether this works or not, what can it hurt?" I gently placed the rose on the threshold. Next to it, I laid down the old queen-of-clubs playing card that I picked up that day. Along with the black rose and playing card, I also left a poem written especially for her.

This may all seem a little bizarre, but whatever it took, I had to put this whole thing to rest once and for all. I whispered softly, *"Rest in peace, Cuban Queen."* I guess it was just my way of saying good-bye. I hoped it would remove this strange allure I had for her. As I turned my back and walked away, I had this tranquil feeling along with an overwhelming sense of relief. Then, unexpectedly, I could faintly smell fried chicken, and then a slight breeze with the sweet scent of rose perfume filled the air. My eyes began to water and that's when I knew it was just her way of saying farewell to me.

A Black Rose for the Cuban Queen

Fare-thee-well O' Cuban Queen,
A black beauty like you was seldom seen.
Free thy hollow heart of pain,
Though the scars of your deeds remain,
I place a black rose at your door,
You're free from the shadows forever more.

Fare-thee-well O' Cuban Queen Bordello,
You've entertained many a lonely fellow.
Free their souls from the whispering tongue,
They're paying now for the wrong they've done.
I place a black rose at your door,
You're free from the shadows forever more.

Fare-thee-well you're now unslaved from shame,
There is no one left living here to blame.
The Jazz music lives on created by Jelly Roll,
You no longer have a royalty on his soul.
I place a black rose at your door,
You're free from the shadows forever more.

Fare-thee-well you're free to travel to worlds unknown
Where they still welcome hearts of stone
The child you took and renamed Henry Ford,
Now rests peacefully with the Lord.
I place a black rose at your door,
You're free from the shadows forever more.

Fare-thee well, this black rose is a gift to you,
There is nothing left here for you to pursue
The walls have confessed to the wrong they've seen.
Please now, Rest in Peace O' Cuban Queen.
I place a black rose at your door,
You're free from the shadows forever more.

Peggy Hicks

It's been a few years since I left that rose on the doorstep of The Cuban Queen's Bordello. The jury is still out on whether or not the black rose was my ticket to freedom from any spell or voodoo curse. At least my life has appeared to return to normal. I've taken a break from the world of real estate, and I now own a small retail store on Jerome's Main Street. Yes, what's left of the old Cuban Queen Bordello building is still standing there in the old red-light district of Jerome. How long the building will continue to stand in the blazing *Ghost City* sun, no one knows. Funny thing though, as fate would have it, as I look out the entrance of my new-found business enterprise, I can clearly see the Cuban Queen's front door just two blocks away. Once in a while on a clear night, I can see a slight twinkle coming from one of the upstairs windows. It's probably just a car's headlight or maybe a star reflecting off some broken glass. But maybe, just maybe it's the sparkle of a diamond, Jelly Roll's diamond, now coming from the shameful grin of the late Cuban Queen herself!

Many have reported paranormal phenomena including the feeling of being watched, the sounds of phantom footsteps, a persistent odor of perfume, and strange shadows that move around at night. Some say, while visiting the historic red-light district, you can still hear the voices of soiled doves calling out from their long vanished cribs.

So, if you find yourself poking around this haunted building known as The Cuban Queen Bordello, don't be alarmed if you see a twinkle of light, or hear a small child crying for its mother. If you suddenly hear jazz music and notice the smell of fried chicken or the scent of rose perfume, don't be frightened. It's just the ghost of The Cuban Queen Bordello.